1

Analyzing the Gospels
בחינות על הבשורות הנוצרים
By Xus Casal

3

"This book is an invitation to the world to make Peace.
Yasher Koakh (congratulations) for all this knowledge and wisdom"

Ariel Cohen Alloro ‖ author of "Ymakh Shmo" ‖ Israel 2015 (5775)

CONTENTS

CHAPTER I: The Gospels

(1.1) Preface

Many others have extensively written on this subject, but I thought necessary to join them due to the many queries that are continuously sent my way. This essay is a small compilation of answers, product of years of study, research and critical analysis as part of the greater mission of ending the generational baseless hatred between Christianity and Judaism. The main issue we are going to deal with is the proper way to approach the Gospels in the so called "New Testament" (N"T). It is not my intention to bombard the reader with unnecessary information or extensive explanations, so this work can be considered an overview.

(1.2) What are the Gospels

Gospel [heb. *besorah*] or **Evangelion** means "annunciation" or "good tidings",[1] and it is the name given by tradition to a collection of books that narrate the life and teachings of the famous master of Galilee, Yeshua (a.k.a Jesus) of Nazareth. If we count all the Gnostic, Christian and Jewish material, there have been found more than 50 different Gospels.
Most of them were considered spurious inventions, made with the intention to make Yeshua fit certain religious agenda, but there is a historical track which leads us to the ones that come from his direct followers - including some that did not make it to the Catholic canon.

(1.3) the authoritative Gospels

(Note: The following information is given in order to trace back the original Gospels, so the theological inclinations of the following people result irrelevant for our purpose.)

• There are those who attribute the canonization of the N"T to the Christian Council of Trullan (692 CE) and others to the Council convened by the Roman emperor Constantine: The Nicea's Council[2] (325 CE), and although there is some truth to the latter, the authority of the canonical or 'authoritative' Gospels (together with the letters of Paul)[3] were not in dispute among the majority of believers, and can be traced back to the 1st Century.[4]

• Most apocryphal Gospels fell into disuse and eventually disappeared. Obviously, the fact that the emperor Constantine and the bishop Athanasius (367 CE) commanded to burn the books they considered 'un-orthodox' had also a lot to do with their disappearance.[5] One who believes in the word of God might say that Divine Providence was behind all this, because by Divine Providence we have the Torah, the Prophets and the words of our sages as we have

---

[1] In Samuel, Gospels are told when an enemy of the king died (*cf. 2S 18 & 4:10*). In Isaiah the Gospel is Israel's redemption from the exile and a global knowledge of God (*cf. 40, 41, 52:7*). In our case, the principal source comes from Isaiah 61:1, where it is written that "the Lord anointed me (משח i.e. has made me Messiah משיח) to give good tidings to the meek…freedom for the captives, etc" which Yeshua applies to himself in his first public shiur (*Luke 4:18*). This annunciation includes the message of repentance (*Mark 1:15*) which is determinant for hastening the Redemption: "If they are worthy, I will hasten it, if not, at the due time" (*cf. Sanhedrin 98a on Is 60:22*).
[2] cf. Pelikan, Jaroslav (2005). *Whose Bible Is It?*.
[3] cf. Gamble, Harry Y, "18", *The Canon Debate, p. 300, note 21*.
[4] Most scholars agree that at least 7 out of the 13 Pauline epistles are unquestionably authentic (*cf. Pheme Perkins, "Reading the New Tetament" pp. 4-7*).
[5] Socrates, "*Church History*" 1:9.30; Athanasius, "*Defense of the Nicene Definition*" 39. cf. Pagels, "*beyond belief: the secret Gospel of Thomas*".

them today, and by Divine Providence each generation receives the books they need to receive. Even the mere existence of Christianity and Judaism are part of Divine Providence.[6]

• **From 120 to 180 CE**, we have sources evidencing the existence of Gospels in both Aramaic and Greek. For instance, Justin Martyr (c. 155 CE) says that it was customary to read on Sundays the books of the Prophets and also the Gospels which he calls: 'memoirs of the apostles' (*First Apology, 67:3*).

• **By the years 160-172 CE,** Tatian (a Syrian Gnostic) composed the Diatessaron; an Aramaic harmonization of 4 Gospels (namely: Matthew, Mark, Luke and John). According to Eusebious the same Tatian rejected Acts but paraphrased Paul (cf. *Hist. Eccl. IV:29:5-6*).

• In the year **140 CE** Marcion 'the heretic' rejected the Hebrew Bible and anything Jewish and composed his own Biblical canon, based on material that was common to Eastern and Western Christians; namely some letters of Paul and his adulterated version of Luke.[7] How did he call this canon? "The New Testament" – a name that ironically remains until today. The Christians in that time acknowledged Marcion's changes on Luke but didn't deny Luke or Paul's authenticity.[8]

• Ireneaus (**180 CE**) in his explanation of the tetramorph mentions by name the four Gospels: Mark, Luke, John and Matthew[9], and gives us a tradition concerning who wrote each Gospel.[10] Such tradition dates back to Papias,[11] the overseer of Hierapolis (95-120 CE); who at the same time cites from his teacher Yohanan the elder (a.k.a John the Presbyter).[12] He had said that Mark was the interpreter of Peter (Keifa)[13] and that Matthew "wrote his narrations in Hebrew language but each one interpreted them as he could" (*Exegesis of the Dominical Logia*).

The common critical estimated date of the Gospels is as follows:[14]

Mark: c.   65-70   CE
Matthew: c.   80-85   CE
Luke: c.   85-90   CE
John: c.   90-110   CE[15]

(1.4) The other Gospels

In addition to the 4 canonical, there were other Gospels known and believed to be reliable by the different Christian sects:

• The "**Gospel of the Hebrews**" – seems to be the name of one or two books[16] coming from an alternative Jewish source. It is said to pertain to the Ebionites; an Essenic[17] Jewish sect[18] that

---

[6] Rambam (*in Hilkhot Melakhim uMilkhamot 11:4*) offers this same perspective concerning Christianity and Islam; with all their errors and mistaken theologies, they are – he says – "part of God's plan to fill the entire world with the mention of Messiah, Torah, and mitzvot".

[7] *Tertullian, "De praescript." 38*; cf. *Ireneaus, "Adversus Haereses 3:12" [3:10.27:2-4]*.

[8] Whether the Pauline epistles we have today were manipulated by Marcion or not is still a subject of debate among the scholars. Many say they were.

[9] *Adversus Haereses 3:11:8*.

[10] *ibid 3:1; cf. Ecclesiastical History 3:39:15-16*.

[11] cf. *Norelli, Enrico (2005). Papia di Hierapolis, Esposizione degli Oracoli del Signore: I frammenti. pp. 38–54*.

[12] cf. *Eusebious: Eccl. Hist. III 39 cf. Adv. Haer. 5:33:4*.

[13] See Eusebious (*Eccl. Hist. 6:14:6-7*) where it is stated that the community requested of Mark to transcribe the sayings of Peter, although Peter himself felt indifferent about it.

[14] cf. *Stephen Harris: Understanding the Bible*. Some scholars even accept dates earlier than these, dating Mark as early as the year 55 CE and Matthew the 60 CE; thus alleging to precede the destruction of the Temple (*cf. Michael Grant: Jesus: an historian's review, pp. 183-189*).

[15] Among the manuscripts, some fragments of John predate the Diatessaron (*e.g. Papyrus Rylands 457*).

[16] The fathers of the Church sometimes confuse one sect with another, so this name probably refers to more than one book.

believed in Yeshua's messiahship mostly by oral transmission, and did not use any 'Christian' book other than the "Gospel of the Ebionites" – which some believe is an alternative form of Matthew.[19] It is also said to have been used by Egyptian Jews until the 4th Century. Citations and references remain, but the book has been completely lost in our days.[20]

• The "**Gospel of Thomas**" is a book of mystical sayings meant for an inner circle, according to most scholars, containing sayings that predate the other gospels, originally in Aramaic and then translated into Greek and Coptic (where Gnostic material was probably added into the text). Despite the popular label of 'Gnostic book', scholars agree that it is not Gnostic and that it predates Christian-Gnosticism.[21] I nevertheless understand why it is easily mistaken for Gnostic literature, as it has traces of an early Hassidic Judaism.[22]

• The are more than 50 books that have been catalogued as "**Gnostic Gospels**", many of them from an early date (c. 140-200 CE). It is mostly agreed among scholars that this literature was written by different sects of Hellenic and/or Jewish-influenced Gnostics (although some may have been wrongly labelled). Apparently, the authors of the Gnostic doctrine (which can be found in books such as the "Trimorphic Protennoia") saw in Yeshua their main source of inspiration. These "hidden" books were read in inner circles, even in Christian monasteries, but are not considered part of any mainstream Christianity, as they are based on Yeshua's secret teachings that deal with attaining spiritual enlightenment (or Messianic consciousness) by meditating on certain spiritual messages that are at times too abstract or too mystical for the common people. Among these we can find "Pistis Sophia", or the gospels of "Philip", "Judas" or "Truth".

• **The different branches of what later became Catholic Christianism** had also a long list of Gospels, such as "the Gospel of James" (145 CE), "the Infancy Gospel of Thomas" (150 CE), "Nativitate Sanctae Mariae" (9th century CE).... etc., all of them written in order to fill the gaps left by the Gospels, especially during Yeshua's infancy. They are also used to prove the Catholic doctrine of Immaculate Conception, but these books are not reliable; they are the Christian equivalent to a Jewish Legend (aggadah), having little or nothing of historical value.

(1.5) the Gospels' reliability

In response to the question about the historicity of the Gospels, the historical evidence supports the idea that at least two Gospels – Mark and Matthew – were globally known a few years after having been written, and Luke (used by Marcion and Tatian) followed them very closely. These were popularly accepted as coming from reliable sources – the tradition of the Master of Galilee was very well known then, and the historical gap is not big enough to deny the possibility of first-hand eyewitnesses.

Before these, we have earlier sources confirming the information; namely, the letters of Paul (*cf. 1Co 15:3-9, 11-12*), the letters of the Disciples (*cf. 1P 2:23-24*), and probably the Gospel of Thomas. In addition, the community of believers wrote for the gentiles a rulebook known as the Didache (c. 70 CE). The Gospel of John came later, and in the second Century was believed to be part of

---

[17] cf. *Hans-Joachim Schoeps; Jewish Christianity: factional disputes in the early church.*

[18] cf. *Adversus Haereses 1:26, 2:21.*

[19] cf. *Epiphanius Pan. Haed. 28:5:1 about the Gospel of Cerinthus.*

[20] According to Eusebious it was "the especial delight of those of the Hebrews who have accepted Christ" (*Ecclesiastical History 3:25:5*).

[21] cf. *Layton, Bentley, The Gnostic Scriptures, 1987, p.361. Davies, Stevan L, The Gospel of Thomas and Christian Wisdom, 1983, pp. 23–24.* Some sentences in the Stromata of Clement of Alexandria are apparently paraphrasing Thomas.

[22] Scholars such as Gershom Scholem postulate that the early origins of Gnosticism were highly influenced not only by Neo-Platonism but mostly by a form of proto-Gnostic Judaism known as the secrets of Heikhalot – today known as Kabbalah (*cf. Scholem, Jewish Gnosticism, Merkabah mysticism, and the Talmudic tradition; cf. Moshe Idel, Kabbalah: New Perspectives p.31*)

the authoritative Gospels by both the fathers of the Church (from whom Christian Orthodoxy would come) and the Gnostics. However, there were communities that rejected the books attributed to John; their opponents called them 'Alogi' or alogians (*cf. Panarion books I & II*).

All scholars agree that the Gospels are compilations of oral traditions. People around the Middle East were talking about the Nazarene and passing the information and stories from mouth to mouth, some of which might have been written down, giving rise to proto-Gospels: this is what scholars call the "Q source" (an inexistent proto-Gospel that theoretically Luke and Matthew might have used as a source). But the origin of all the sources is the oral transmission and that is evident.

Why did the Gospels (until then only known in oral form) require to be written down 30-50 years after the actual events? This was a time when riots and insurrections led to the destruction of Jerusalem. This was one of those time periods where all sects of Judaism did the exact same thing: writing down their oral traditions for the fear of losing them in the exile.[23]

The Talmudist Yosef Klausner says about the Gospels: "We are not to look them for naked, unadorned history: they are compilations, religious in their nature, seeking to portrait the messianic character of Yeshua" (*Yeshua miNaztaret pg. 81*). Considering, then, that the Gospels are not history books, the critical information they serve is solid: In the first century people knew a Jewish Rabbi called Yeshua who taught very deep teachings by which he made a good number of followers, performed wonders, died hanged on a tree by the Romans and rose from the dead. Paul even says that if this did not happen "then our preaching is vain" (*1Co 15:14*), because in his days there were eyewitnesses of such events to whom he knew personally; one of them being Yeshua's brother himself (*cf. Gal 1:19; 1Co 15:6*).

• First Century references to Yeshua are also found in the historians Tacitus (*Annals 15:44*)[24] and Josephus (*Antiquities 20:9.1*),[25] and critical (even atheist) scholars almost universally agree that at least the baptism, the issue at the Temple, and the crucifixion are historical events.[26]

• The above is a nuisance to those who claim that Yeshua never existed based on what they call "lack of evidences".[27] Actually there is more evidence of his existence than of any other

---

[23] The Mishna, the Jerusalem Talmud, Agadot, the texts of the Essenes, Maasei Merkava literature, Sefer Yetzirah, the Bahir, etc... all began to be written down in times where all that knowledge could be lost; either after the death of Alexander the Great *(323 BCE)*, during the wars for the division of Israel *(198 BCE to 63 BCE)*, after the destruction of Israel *(70 CE)*, or after the final Roman exile *(136 CE onward)*.

[24] Few scholars suggested that the reference is spurious, but the overwhelming majority dismissed the idea and treat it as an authentic reference to Yeshua (cf. Craig A. Evans, *"Jesus and his contemporaries" p. 42*; Helen K. Bond, *"Pontius Pilate in history and interpretation" p. xi*; Robert E Van Voorst *"Jesus outside the New Testament" pp. 39-53*).

[25] "Now there was about this time Jesus, a wise man, a teacher. He drew over to him both many of the Jews and many of the Gentiles. Pilate had condemned him to the cross, but those that loved him at the first did not forsake him. They informed that he had appeared to them and was alive, and that he was possibly the Messiah about whom our prophets spoke wonders" (*Josephus, Antiquities 18:3, as per Agapios "Kitab al-unwan"*). Greek manuscripts seem to include Christian additions that are not found in the Arab version. Nevertheless, most scholars consider Yeshua's reference as absolutely authentic (*cf. John Drane, "introducing New Testament" p. 138; Dr. James H. Charlesworth, "Jesus within Judaism" p. 96*). Josephus also mentions Yaakov, Yeshua's brother, two chapters later (cf. *Antiquities 20:9.1*).

[26] cf. *Mark Allan Power "Jesus as a figure in history" pp. 168-173; Crossan "Jesus; a revolutionary biography" p. 145; Van Voorst "Jesus Outside the New Testament", p. 16.*

[27] Conspiracy theorists, anti-missionary mythicists...etc mostly relying on the work of a Protestant theologian known as Rudolf Karl Bultmann (a work that has been refuted by many other scholars). They make great efforts to try and disprove each and every evidence of a historical Yeshua; something they never do with any other historic figure.

religious leader of the past. Because apart from traditions and faith, what physical proofs do we have that Abraham, Moses, Buddha, Lao-Zi or many others existed? Even in the case of king David, until a few decades ago we had no evidence of his existence, and then an archaeological artefact was discovered with the supposed inscription: "Beit David". Not having enough evidence for an irrefutable proof has never been a reason to reject ancient historical figures, how much more so when Yeshua is directly mentioned in earlier sources and the Gospels are quite closer to his time than the writings of other religious figures? The scholar and historian Michael Grant says:

> "If we apply to the New Testament, as we should, the same sort of criteria as we should apply to other ancient writings containing historical material, we can no more reject Jesus' existence than we can reject the existence of a mass of pagan personages whose reality as historical figures is never questioned"
> (*Grant: Jesus; an historian's review pp. 199-200*).

• I would go further and say that denying the existence of Yeshua is denying our very Jewish tradition. The Talmud mentions that Eliezer ben Hurcanos was pleased with the words that a Nazarene taught him as coming from Yeshua's mouth (*cf. Avoda Zara 17a; Qohelet Rabbah on 1:8*), and the midrashim regard Shimon Keifa [28] and Yaakov the Just (Yeshua's brother) as tzaddiqim (i.e., saints).[29] In fact, according to a Jewish tradition it was Shimon Keifa who composed the 'Nishmat' and one of the 'Yom Kippur' prayers (cf. *Rabbeinu Tam; Mahzor Vitri p. 285; see also Epiphanius "Anacephalaiosis" 15:1*).

(1.6) the Textual Variations

Concerning the accuracy of transmission and the preservation of the original texts:
• There are differences between the more than 20,000 manuscripts [30] found, which is understandable considering the work involved in the copy of manuscripts. When a book was sent to a new region, it was copied there, again and again by scribes – who sometimes committed errors, or wrote on the margins, or corrected parts of the text that did not need to be corrected. Thank God, we have so many manuscripts that the variations are traceable. Almost all changes have to do with grammar, punctuation, spelling and local expressions. There are few instances, though, where the variations involve a theological agenda and pretend to support spurious theology – this explains why there are so many later interpolations as well – in these cases one requires scholarly research and critical analysis. Notwithstanding, based on the old manuscripts, the translations and the quotes of the early theologians, one can say that the text has been fairly preserved.
• Based on the above, the three major textual families among the Greek manuscripts are the Alexandrian[31], the Western[32] and the Byzantine.[33] In addition to these there is the Eastern

---

[28] Shimon Keifa; also known as Peter in the Western World.
[29] cf. *Otzar haMidrashim al Nakh*. cf. *Rav Yehuda haHassid "sefer Hassidim" 191, p. 85*.
[30] "A study of 150 Greek manuscripts of Luke has revealed more than 30,000 different readings… It is safe to say that there is not one sentence in the New Testament in which the manuscript is wholly uniform" (*M. M Parvis, vol 4, pp. 594-595 – Interpreter's dictionary of the Bible*).
[31] The Alexandrian family is believed to reflect earlier readings. The most representative of these manuscripts are the Bodmer Papyri (c. 200), the Codex Vaticanus (c. 300) and the Codex Sinaiticus (c. 330).
[32] In the Western the text is enlarged and paraphrased, while in specific places is quite shorter than the Alexandrian. The Codex Bezae (c. 400) is the most representative.
[33] Byzantine texts are later critical copies of older manuscripts. The codex Alexandrinus (c. 400) and the codex Ephraemi Rescriptus (c. 420) are the most representative. In general, Byzantine readings represent the Catholic traditional preference.

tradition recorded in Aramaic material, such as the Aramaic Peshitta (435 C.E.).[34] Almost every fragment found[35] can be catalogued as corresponding to one of these traditions.[36]

• The so-called Old Syriac Gospels (syr^{cur} & syr^s), approximately dated back to the 4th Century CE, are Aramaic manuscripts that seem to follow an earlier reading. These manuscripts lack several of the spurious interpolations, such as the last 12 verses of Mark, the reconciliation between Herod and Pilate in Luke (*Lk 23:10-12*) and the story of the adulteress in John (*Jn 7:53-8:11*), and also contain alternative readings in some verses. This is a very important material for a critical analysis.[37]

We do not really know the story behind the Old Syriac; some suggest they reflect the original Gospels or the ones quoted by Hegessipus in the 2nd century, others say it is a (mis)translation and others say they were created and used by some heretic sect. The only thing we know for certain is that **Divine Providence** wanted the Gospels to reach us in their current form.

(1.7) My textual preference

• Why do my colleagues and I prefer the Peshitta if I am not a Peshitta primacist?
  (a) Because the Gospels are Jewish literature. The Talmud, Targumim, Midrashim, Zohar… are all written in Hebrew and Aramaic. Why shouldn't we follow the Syrian instead of the Roman tradition?[38] After all, we have seen (in point 1.6) that there is no Divine Inspiration whatsoever in the arrangement of the Greek words.
  (b) Because Divine Providence has smiled on the Peshitta's face in that it has remained unchanged for more than 15 hundred years[39] (unlike the Greek).
  (c) Because the Peshitta solves many instances where Greek manuscripts differ.

Let us see together an example:

■ In Mark 1:41, majority sources say that Yeshua was: "**moved with compassion**"[40]; however, the Codex Bezae and a couple Latin translations read that he "**was moved with anger**"[41]. The dilemma of the scholars is obvious: If the original reading is 'moved with compassion' why in the world would any scribe want to change it to be 'moved with anger'? Compassion and anger are antonyms, sound completely different, and there is no theological reason for the

---

[34] The Peshitta agrees with the Textus Receptus 108 times, with the Codex Vaticanus 65 times and in 137 occasions it contradicts both, agreeing with alternative readings such as the Old Syriac and 31 times with a seemingly unique reading (*cf. Bruce M. Metzger*).

[35] Every fragment; including Latin, Arabic and Coptic translations. There are cases where the fragments reflect a combination of more than one tradition.

[36] At the end of the 4th Century (382 C.E.), Jerome of Stridon was commanded to translate the Bible into Latin. This (the Vulgate) became the official Bible of the Catholic Church (*cf. Council of trent, 1545-63*). Meanwhile, they worked on a critical reconstruction of the Greek text, known as the Textus Receptus (1512 CE onward), which was used (together with the Vulgate) to translate the Bibles into English, German, Spanish… etc. There are some that make the absurd claim that this is an Inspired text, while scholars say it was a botched job.

[37] See for instance the interesting reading in the Syriac Sinaiticus of Matthew chapter 1.

[38] Eastern Community "believe according to their traditions that the Peshitta (Aramaic Canon of the New Testament) is the original text" (*cf. Mar Eshai Shimun XXIII*). Eusebious seems to hint to this when he said that "Hegesippus [an Eastern Nazarene] quoted the gospel according to the Hebrews and from the Syriac [Aramaic N"T] and from the [Jewish] oral tradition" (*Eusebious, 160 C.E., hist. Eccles. IV 22:8*).

[39] Thomas of Harqel (616 C.E) translated into Aramaic the books that are not part of the Eastern cannon (*2Peter, 2-3 John, Jude & Revelation*); but the Harqlean Version did not actually replace the Peshitta.

[40] Splagchnistheis; σπλαγχνισθεὶς.

[41] Orgistheis; οργισθεις.

change! [42] According to scholars [43] the Syriac word for "having compassion" (Ethrakham אתרחם)[44] can be easily confused with the word for 'getting angry' (Ethra'am אתרעם).[45]

Here there are a few other examples:

■ Matthew 6:1, "your alms" or "your righteousness"? Greek manuscripts differ,[46] some say 'alms' some say 'righteousness'. The Peshitta uses 'b'Zidqatkhon' בזדקתכון from the root 'zedeq' זדק. Zedqata זדקתא is the equivalent to the Hebrew Tzedaqah (צדקה). This word evolved from specifically meaning 'righteousness' to meaning 'charity', so it can mean both.

■ Luke 7:35 [cf. Mt 11:19], is it "her sons" or "her works"? Again, Greek versions differ. In Luke, the Peshitta uses 'Bneiah' בניה which can mean both. How so? Well, the last letter (ה) turns the word into a possessive; so if one reads the word literally as בני (plural of בר) we got: "her children" but if we read it as coming from the root בנא (to build, to work on something) we could read: "her works".[47]

■ Luke 7:45, is it "since I came in" or "since she came in"? The Peshitta uses 'd'Elat' דעלת which can be read both ways (see for instance 'Elat' in Acts 5:7).

■ John 11:31, is it "they were thinking" or "they were saying"? The Peshitta uses 'sebaro' סברו which means 'they assumed', thus harmonizing both ideas.

The Peshitta harmonizes many discrepancies between the Greek manuscripts; it leads one to believe that there is an Aramaic original source underlying all the different versions.
Of course, the Peshitta primacists think this is an evidence that the Peshitta is the original text of the New Testament, but I disagree. In my opinion the Peshitta is the result of having altered an original Aramaic text in order to harmonize it with the Greek Byzantine texts of the 4th century. [48]

---

[42] The change is so absurd that some scholars offer homiletic explanations to support the belief that the Codex Bezae had the original reading, but this opinion hangs by a thread.

[43] cf. *Bruce Metzger: "A textual commentary on the Greek New Testament"*, 2nd edition p. 56 [77].

[44] In Syriac characters: ܐܬܪܚܡ from the Heb. root רחם; compassion, pity or bowels.

[45] In Syriac characters: ܐܬܪܥܡ from the Ar. noun: רועמא ; indignation, disagreement or righteous anger.

[46] Δικαιοσυνην (justice) [e.g. *in* א] and ελεημοσυνην (alms) [e.g. *in C (04)*].

[47] I would be inclined to read it as 'her children' but the intended meaning is "her works", as Matthew corroborates using unmistakably 'avodeiah' עבדיה i.e. 'her works' (*Mt 11:19*).

[48] It is because of this that when I say we prefer the Peshitta over the Greek, I don't mean at all that we have it canonized as the original and perfect text, but rather, that we find it very valuable in matters of critical study and in the reconstruction of that possible original Aramaic text, together with the Hebrew thought, which clearly underlies the N"T.

CHAPTER 2: The Jewish authors

Some would argue that the Gospels have been in gentile hands from the beginning and that they are not teaching Judaism. After all, they are the Holy Bible of the Christians.
While it is true that they fell in Christian and Gnostic hands, their content demonstrates that we are not reading Christian or Gnostic literature. No scholar would ever deny that the Gospels are the product of a Jewish sect,[49] and that despite its acceptance of gentiles, the sect in the beginning remained Jewish.[50] Yet, the keepers[51] of the authoritative Gospels and their Messiah are gentiles who built from them a totally new religion and theology due to not having the proper tools to interpret them.

• Christianity claims that they not only inherited the books, but also the 'divine tradition' and the 'authority to interpret them', but a scholarly comparison between Gospels and 'Church' theology tells otherwise.
Eusebious, for instance, being a father of the church and an influential character in Christendom,[52] allegedly affirmed not having any knowledge of Aramaic, Hebrew, or Jewish traditions,[53] so how can he properly interpret what is taking place in the Gospels? How will he understand the meaning of key expressions that the writers did not even bother to explain? His theology, then, is built upon foreign ideas, it does not make any sense to follow "his" Gospel.[54]

• The Gospels were certainly written by Jews, but most Christian interpretations verge on anti-Semitism because they isolate the Gospels from their religious, historical and geographical context.[55] Although the New Testament has no validity whatsoever without the Jewish texts that shape them, many have even dared to say that it is not necessary to read the Hebrew Scriptures (what they naively call: Old Testament"), even though Yeshua's disciples said about them that they are: "Living words for us" (*Acts 7:38*).

This raises the question: Why Christianity and Judaism began to walk in different paths? According to scholars there were many - smaller and bigger - reasons for it, especially during the first years. Many scholars directly blame Paul for teaching a theology that was against the principles of the Nazarene community, represented in Yaqov the Just (Yeshua's brother) and even in Keifa (aka Peter). Some Jewish scholars such as Mark Nanos disagree, because - according to them - Paul's letters addressed people who gathered yet in Synagogues and followed a Jewish community system, so those texts cannot be understood without contextualizing each and every letter separately. It is noteworthy nevertheless that even in

---

[49] "What we learned from the Gospel stories is not that Jesus was not Jewish. Quite the opposite. He's completely embedded in the Judaism of his time" (*Paula Frediksen, Boston University: From Jesus to Christ part 1*). "Was Jesus a Jew?.... He was born, lived, died, taught as a Jew" (*Shaye J.D. Cohen: From Jesus to Christ part 1*).

[50] "At the end of the 1st century AD there were not yet two separate religions called 'Judaism' and 'Christianity'" (*Robert Goldenberg, review of 'dying for God and the making of Christianity and Judaism' by Daniel Boyarin in the Jewish Qarterly review, vol 92, pp. 586-588*).

[51] Keepers, Heb. **נוצרים**. In Semitic languages Christians are known by this word.

[52] cf. *Sozomen, "Eccl. Hist." I:8, 19.*

[53] cf. *C. J. Elliot "Hebrew learning among the fathers".*

[54] I would say that, on the contrary, he (and most of the Church fathers) would misinterpret the text based on Roman mythology and Greek philosophy which were their major influence.

[55] The father of protestant theology, Martin Luther, went as far as saying, "what shall we Christians do with this rejected and condemned people, the Jews?... first, to set fire to their synagogues... I advise that their houses also be razed and destroyed... [because they are]... a brood of vipers and sons of the devil" (*Luther, "On the Jews and their lies", pp. 268-278, or "Von den Juden und ihren Lügen"*).

Paul's letters we find gentiles who saw themselves as replacing the unbelieving Jews (*Rom 11:18-27*), so in this sense, the separation began as early as Paul began teaching Torah to the gentiles (who in most cases just came out of paganism and did not have a Torah foundation). However, among the many historical situations that caused the separation between Christianity and Judaism, one of the major events was certainly the **third Jewish revolt against Rome** (c. 132-136 CE), where Jews and Yeshua's followers - as one single religious group - were massacred in a genocide[56] and expelled from Jerusalem.[57] In that time separation began due to Bar Kokhva's arrogant Messianic self-proclamation.[58] This leader of the rebellion was such a bloodthirsty dictator[59] that even "commanded Christians to be severally punished if they did not deny Yeshua as Messiah and blaspheme him" (*Justin, First Apology 31:5-6*); thus causing Christians to completely depart from the tree that had been nourishing them.

The so-called Fathers of the Church began to see Christianity as a religion for gentiles (*Origen contra Celsus VII:26*), perceiving Judaism sometimes as an exclusive religion for Jews, and sometimes as a withered religion that Christianity had begun to replace. The Jewish Rabbi Yaqov Emden saw in Christianity (as defined in the NT) a Noahide movement (i.e. a movement for gentiles, but within the rules and endorsement of Judaism) which broke down and went astray because of a lack of Jewish leadership. We will come back to this topic later (*in chapter 10; see also note 110*).

One thing is clear: the closer one gets to the Gospels, the further one goes from modern Christian theology, and the closer one gets to Judaism. I plan to briefly expound Jesus' Judaism as depicted in the Gospels, but before that, I believe necessary to tackle some other topics that, hopefully, will offer a little contextual background.

---

[56] cf. *Totten S. "Teaching about genocide p. 24".*

[57] cf. *Linda Davinson, "Pilgrimage: From the ganges to graceland: an Enciclopedia, Vol. 1"* (cf. *Eccl. Hist. IV:6:3*).

[58] cf. *Eusebious, Eccl. Hist. IV:6:1-2*; cf. *Yerushalmi Taanit 4:5.*

[59] "Bar Kokhva... had with him two hundred thousand men with an amputated finger. The Sages sent him the message, 'How long will you continue to make the men of Israel blemished?" (*Eikha Rabbah 2.2,4*).

CHAPTER 3: Overview on the Gospels

(3.1) Are the Gospels missionary?

It has been widely assumed that the three synoptic Gospels were created with the intention to evangelize, or to convert people to Christianity. That cannot be the case because:

(a) Christianity as the religion we know today did not exist when the Gospels were written down; the sect of the Nazarenes belonged to Judaism.

(b) 90% of the material in the Gospels are preachings, sermons and details about Yeshua that prove nothing of his messiahship; evangelization cannot be the main purpose of these books.

(c) If they were intended for converting a Jewish audience, their content is homiletically debatable and easily refutable, and if to heathens, the content is meaningless since they did not care about the Jewish Bible. The 'evidences' only make sense to the initiated.

(d) Specifically Luke, in the introduction of his book declares that his intention is to organize traditions about Yeshua that were being taught among the believers (*Luk. 1:3*).

In the following paragraphs let's briefly examine how each Gospel presents its content and what can we learn about the writers.

(3.2) About Mark

Of the Synoptic Gospels, Mark is the earliest. Messianics refer to the Gospel of Mark as the **Besorah al Pi haPeshat** (the Gospel according to its literal level of interpretation), and I understand why. Mark is the most straight-forward of the Gospels. He simply records the tradition as he received it without adding any further opinion or midrashic explanation.[60]

Mark's Greek is very poor, in fact the worst, as far as Greek Biblical literature is concerned, and at times it makes use of common Latin words (*5:9; 6:27, 37; 12:42; 15:16*).

There are few instances in the *Koine* manuscripts where the narration is interrupted with clarifications of Jewish words or a Jewish tradition (*3:17; 5:41; 7:11, 34; 14:36; 15:22*).[61] This indicates that probably the author and the final audience of the Greek manuscripts were gentiles; maybe Romans.

It cannot be ignored that in Mark there are many accounts where Yeshua's references to the Tanakh[62] are taken from[63] Aramaic Sources[64] (cf. *1:15; 4:12, 9:47-48; 12:1-12*).

(3.3) Mark and the Sea of Galilee

As mentioned above, the traditional view states that the Gospel was the product of Mark recording the sayings of Keifa (a.k.a Peter). This is very difficult to demonstrate but a few scholars[65] find traces of this claim in the confused Markan geography. The Gospel gives a detailed and precise list of the geographical locations where Yeshua travelled, but it is very

---

[60] There are a few exceptions (*such as verse 15:28*) where later scribes added verses from Luke or Matthew, but those verses are not part of the original text.

[61] It also happens in John, in an absurd incident in which a Samaritan teaches Yeshua that Messiah means "anointed" (*John 4:25*). One concludes that these clarifications were added by translators.

[62] TaNaKh, acronym for: Torah + Neviim + Ketuvim; i.e. the Hebrew Bible.

[63] His quotes agree or follow the same style with the Targumim (*see next note*).

[64] After the reading of the Torah in the Synagogue, it was customary since the time of Ezra and Nehemiah to give or read Aramaic interpretations (i.e. Targumim) (*Neh 8:8*). Targum means 'translation'.

[65] Prof. Richard Bauckham, '*Mark's Geography and the origin of Mark's Gospel*'.

complicated to make sense of the journeys and trace them into a map, especially in the Galilean chapters; one could easily say the places are chaotic and even erroneous. The solution comes when we do not think of Mark's itinerary in cartographic terms – after all, he more than likely did not have reference books or a map – instead, he had a functional cognitive map of the area which is the way all common people of that time perceived their environment. Today's mental maps are very contaminated with the cartographic maps, but in the past that was not the case, especially in areas where one travelled regularly. Ask different people to describe for you an itinerary from one place to another without a map, and the answers will surprisingly vary based on their personal orientation point and how they perceive their environment.

Yeshua met Keifa and his first disciples while they were fishing in the Sea of Galilee (*1:16, 20*), and the first half of Mark's Gospel is largely located around the shores of this lake. Only in other Gospels we learn of places beyond the shore. Yeshua travels the lake (*4:35-36*), even separates himself from the oppressing multitudes getting into a boat (*3:9, 4:1*), and their common meal was fish (probably sardines).

The point being made is that the Gospel of Mark seems to be composed by a fisherman of Kefar-Nahum who offered a mental functional map of those places he was familiar with and Yeshua used to pass by.

(3.4) About Matthew

Both Matthew and Luke supplement Mark from written or oral sources (*cf. Yosef Klausner, Yeshua miNatzaret p. 80*). Matthew adds new traditions and new sermons. Furthermore, he develops these stories, returning to them from a retrospective point of view, giving them homiletic values, similar to what the midrashim do with the Torah text.

It is especially notorious the Sermon of the Mount, where Yeshua cites (at times word by word) teachings of the Pharisees – especially from the school of Hillel, which gives us Yeshua's Jewish background. This also makes us consider the author of the Gospel: tradition says it was originally composed in Hebrew (or Aramaic) by Mattai, one of the twelve disciples. We canont prove that, but the fact that this book was attributed specifically to him practically from its inception is interesting, nonetheless. On the other hand (we have already tackled this) some theorized the "Gospel according to the Hebrews" was the original of Matthew, also named "the Gospel of the Twelve".

Apparently, Matthew seeks to demonstrate that Yeshua is the Messiah by quoting several verses from the Tanakh which he says were fulfilled in Yeshua's lifetime. However, if that was his intention he would have focused on the attributes or events that evidence that Yeshua fits the criteria for being Messiah; he would do so using literal exegesis on actual Messianic prophecies that other Jews could not deny. But instead, he focuses on sermons and parables that demonstrate nothing of Yeshua's messiahship[66] and, as a matter of fact, most of the verses he quotes from the Tanakh are not messianic prophecies, or are not prophecies at all, or simply, do not speak of Messiah in their literal meaning.[67] So why does he quote them?

On its use and attribution of Scriptural quotes to Yeshua (in form of Pesharim, *see note 68*), the book presupposes a background and understanding of Jewish homiletics by both the writer

---

[66] Even his introductory genealogy is filled with homiletic riddles, arranging it intentionally in three sets of 14 names; being that 14 is the Gematria (numerical value) of David דוד.

[67] One of the famous stories is when Herod slew all the children under 2 of Bethlehem and the coasts nearby (*Matt. 2:16*). Matthew claims that this event fulfilled the words of the prophet Jeremiah, but if you read the prophet's verse in context, it is about Israel's exile; not about Messiah's birth (*cf. Jer. 31:15-16*).

and the reader, and consequently expects the new reader to develop the exegetic connection between the Biblical reference and the narration that is taking place. Taking those references as actual or literal prophecies simply damages the composition and causes the Orthodox Jew to reject the book.

No wonder why Messianics say that Matthew is known as **"Besorah al pi haDrash"** (the Gospel according to its homiletic level), because, indeed, one is required to understand that Matthew delves into the **Pesher**[68] (profound visionary interpretation) of the verses.

(3.5) About Luke

Luke is a narration consisting of two books: Luke and Acts. Although anonymous, the idea that Luke wrote this Gospel is based on internal hints of the N"T. Paul talks about a certain Luke who was his close companion (*2Ti 4:11; Col 4:14; Flm 1:24*) and there are several brief sections in the book of Acts where the author narrates Paul's travels in first-person perspective, as if he was a direct eyewitness of those events (*Acts 16:10-17, 20:5-15, 21:1-18, 27:1-28:16*). However, the author never identifies himself as Luke, so we are still relying on Oral Tradition. He calls his Gospel "a diegesis" (i.e. a narration of legends) and claims to be a receiver of those traditions and not an eyewitness (*1:2*); he had been collecting different (written and oral) material about Yeshua – which he says is reliable (*1:1*) – and his main purpose was to organize it (*Luke 1:3; Acts 1:1*). The book is addressed to someone called Theophilus – which some scholars claim (only because of the name) to be a Roman authority. However, there are two points to take into consideration:

(a) There are Jews called Theophilus – for instance Theophilus ben Anas; the High Priest.

(b) Theophilus in Greek means "lover of God" and it might refer to any believer in general.

Messianics say Luke is the **Besorah al Pi haRemez** (Gospel according to its alluded meaning). I cannot find any good reason for it, since Luke uses the same techniques of Matthew, and Matthew uses *Remez* as well. Neither he speaks of Yeshua in hints, quite the opposite. If at all, I would suggest that the book is in itself an allusion to other Gospels:

---

[68] **Pesher** is a method of personal midrashic revelation, especially used in the Qumran community but also in the Zohar and other midrashim. Its name comes from Eccl 8:1 and from Daniel's interpretations [pesharim] of dreams, and is based on the idea that every verse in the Bible conceals a deeper message for the present generation that can be revealed by the righteous Master (cf. *George Brooke: Qumran Pesher: Toward the Redefinition of a Genre. In: Revue de Qumran 10, 483-503*).

The Essenes (ebionites) would probably add that all the prophets spoke only of Yemot haMashiakh – the days of Messiah (*see Sanhedrin 99a [notice it doesn't say "Messiah" but "days of Messiah"; which includes all his footsteps]*). Being that Pesher is a form of midrash, there are midrashim that reflect its characteristics. Let's see the following example:

A midrash (*Tanhuma Toldot*) says that Messiah will be greater than Moses based on the verse (*Num. 11:12*): "that you say to me, carry them in your bosom". While the verse does not speak of Messiah at all, and there seems to be no context for such a claim, this is a deduction based on its homiletic study.

Once Rabbi Huna was attacked by a mad dog and he stripped off his clothes and ran away. According to the Gemara he fulfilled the verse: "wisdom preserves the life of him who has it" (*Yoma 84a*). Similarly, the Zohar applies to Shimon bar Yohai the verse: 'you shall rest in peace, and arise again for your lot at the end of the days' (*Zohar III:296b*) – even though we know the text is talking to Daniel.

When Rabbi Yohanan and his friend Ilfa decided to leave Torah study to find a job because of poverty, they fulfilled the verse: 'there shall be no needy among you' (*Taanit 21a*). Rabbi Israel Ber Oddeser of Breslev said that Rebbe Nahman fulfilled the words of Isaiah: "The world will be filled with the knowledge of God" (*Song of Redemption pg. 31-32*).

In modern times, Rabbis and Kabbalists use **Pesher** for example to identify Adolf Hitler with Amalek, or Edom with Christianity (*cf. Ephraim Oshry, "the Annihilation of Lithuanian Jewry", p. 172; Abarbanel on Ovadiah*).

A 76% of its content is the same with Mark's; and another 23% is shared with Matthew. Only a 35% is new material, including new miracles, new parables and especially more details about Yeshua's infancy.

(3.6) About John

John's reading is quite interesting, since it collectively describes Yeshua's debaters as "the Jews" (as if Yeshua himself was not a Jew). This has led many scholars to believe that the Gospel of John is a highly anti-Semitic Christian composition. The content, though, is radically the opposite. It is in this Gospel that Yeshua says: "salvation is of the Jews". The Gospel uses several methods of Jewish Scriptural interpretation and is familiar with both Judea's geography (Jn 5:2) and Jewish literature (such as the Solomonic books); the main source of the text is therefore Jewish. The best way, then, to solve this paradox is to realize that the term 'Yehudi'[69] can refer to Jews (those who practice Judaism) or to Judeans (those who lived in Judea, as opposed to Samaritans or Galileans). Contextually speaking, most of the times the "Yehudim" appear in the Gospel of John, it refers to Judeans[70] and their mindset and not the Jews in general (comp Jn 7:1, 11:7-19).

About John's historical accuracy, there are two issues: Firstly, the Gospel is mystical in essence (or spiritual[71] if you prefer that term). Secondly, it is a completely different tradition.

John is mystical in essence: it begins with a mystical poem and continues with extensive sermons filled with mystical riddles, and the seemingly historical events in the book are based on seven signs that were done on certain Jewish holidays. John challenges us to see beyond the text;[72] it is obviously not meant for historical accuracy.

Based on the metaphorical expression: "the beloved disciple" (Jn 21:20-24) a tradition attributes the book to John the apostle, but this is simply another spiritual riddle that someone took literally. Of course, the author never identifies himself, and the chances that John actually wrote it are very little. The estimated time of writing is very late (80-110 CE), and the narration has traces of having been written by more than one hand: the Greek text changes its style sometimes and (at least the version we have) contains a great number of late glosses.[73] The words: "This is the disciple which testifies…. and we know that his testimony is true" (Jn 21:24), can be seen as an allusion to the plural authorship of the book. In fact, there is an oral tradition which says that the book is a compilation of revelations that the disciples gathered together after fasting for three days;[74] which brings me to the next point.

It is a completely different tradition: One could say that any similarity with the synoptic Gospels is just the confirmation of a reliable oral tradition. While all the gospels serve a theological and religious purpose, so historical accuracy is just secondary, it is evident that John was intended as a mere spiritual book. For centuries Christian theologians have tried to harmonize the Gospels (some better than others), but it is evident and undeniable that at times

---

[69] Gr. Ιουδαῖοσ; Ar. יהודאי.

[70] cf. Steve Mason, "Jews, Judaeans, Judaizing, Judaism: Problems of Categorization in Ancient History", Journal for the Study of Judaism 38, pp. 1-56. cf. Shaye Cohen, "Ioudaios" 219.

[71] Even the Fathers of the Church call it: "a spiritual Gospel" (cf. Eusebious: Ecclesiastical History 6:14:7).

[72] That is also a characteristic of Thomas, which in no way was intended as a historical book.

[73] such as 5:3b-4, 7:53-8:11 and the whole chapter 21 – which presupposes that Keifa had already died by that time.

[74] "When his fellow disciples and elders were urging him, he said: Fast with me for three days beginning today, and whatever will have been revealed to us, let us recount it with each other" (Muratorian Canon; cf. Faith of the Early Fathers, vol. I, p. 107).

John contradicts the synoptic. [75] The contradictions are intentional though, serving a theological purpose. Still, one of the rules of critical analysis is that the earlier material is likely more reliable.

- In John Yeshua cleanses the Temple at the beginning of his ministry which lasts at least one year more. In the other Gospels the disturbance at the Temple was one of the major reasons for his detention and execution. It happened, necessarily, at the end of his ministry.
- In the synoptic gospels Yeshua meets his two first disciples – Andres and Keifa – in a fishing after his 40 days fasting in the desert (*Mark 1:16; Matt. 4:18; Luke 5:3*). In the book of John he meets Andres and another disciple one day after his baptism, and Keifa is brought later by Andres (*Jn 1:35-41*).
- In the synoptic Gospels Yeshua is arrested after Pesakh[76] (*Mrk 14:12-14,26,46; Lk 22:15*), he clearly celebrates a Passover meal before his detention. But in John he is executed before Pesakh in order to make of Yeshua 'the Lamb of God' (*Jn 1:29; 18:28; 19:31*).
- In the synoptic gospels Yeshua prays with suffering: let this cup pass from me (*Mt 26:39*); he is in such an agonic tension that he sweats drops of blood (*Lk 22:44*). But in John there is no mention of suffering; on the contrary, Yeshua is in total control of the situation (*Jn 18:4*) and when the guards come to arrest him, they fall before him (*Jn 18:6*).
- The main theme of the synoptics is the kingdom of God. In John it seems the main focus is Yeshua himself, who incarnates both the Torah and Messiah's soul.

Do not take me wrong, I am not saying there is no truth in John. What I mean to say is that **(a)** it narrates an independent oral account and **(b)** the book is focused on concealed truths – deeper and mystical things – which should be our focus too when we read it, instead of taking everything at face value. From a critical point of view, chances are many that its historical narration is a legend (aggadah) that serves merely to connect one teaching with the next.[77]
It perfectly fits the name given by Messianics: **Besorah al Pi haSod** (the Gospel according to its secret meaning). This way, each Gospel corresponds to one of the four levels of Jewish exegesis.[78]

In John's narration there are two important characters: one of them is the **beloved disciple**; a figure that appears after the eleventh chapter resting at his master's chest (*Jn 13:23*), staying where others run away (*19:26*), arriving to the sepulchre faster than Keifa (*20:4*), and who remains until Yeshua comes back (*21:23*).[79] He is a metaphor for the perfect believer and the Messianic community. The other figure is **Nicodemus**, a leader Pharisee and member of the Sanhedrin (*7:50*) who incarnates in the Gospels the not-so-well known group of "righteous Pharisees" against whom Yeshua does not target[80] (cf. *Lk 13:31*). His mention by name probably indicates a real 1st century historical figure of renown. We will talk about it.

---

[75] I mean from a critical point of view.
[76] Pesakh; the Hebrew for Passover.
[77] Such is the case in the book of the Zohar, where the narration is an aggadah about Shimon bar Yohai and his students coming up to Jerusalem, and meeting different people in the path. We know that the Zohar was composed by more than one hand in different time periods; yet, we call it 'the Holy Zohar' and attribute all of it to Rav Shimon.
[78] Pshat, Remez, Drash and Sod; called by the acronym of PaRDeS (which means paradise).
[79] Tradition says it is John, and other critical theologians argue that he might be Eleazar (Lazarus), who is the one of whom the Gospel says "Behold how he loved him" (*Jn 11:5, 36*). However, the evidence indicates that this is not the work of one individual.
[80] There is the popular and yet erroneous belief among Christians that the term "Pharisee" equals 'hypocrite' and/or 'legalist' because Yeshua attacked them all. Such a claim is not supported by historical or religious external sources, and not even by the Gospels themselves, as we will see later.

CHAPTER 4: Gospels' religious background

(4.1) Second Temple period

The Gospels make constant allusions to the religious and political situation of Israel in the first century, but the information they offer is quite insufficient for building a proper perspective, so let's begin to make sense of each element.

• The Second Temple era began when the king Cyrus of Persia (515 BCE – 70 CE) allowed the Jews to rebuild Jerusalem and the Temple (*Ezra 1:1-3*).[81]

• The rebuilding of the Temple and the cleansing of pagan assimilation was possible due to the efforts of Nehemiah (*Neh 3:38, 4:15*) and Ezra the scribe (*Ez 7:6, 10*), who created the 'Great Assembly',[82] canonized the Hebrew Bible[83] and began to popularize the relatively new Batei-Knesset (congregational houses; later known as synagogues).

• From the time of Ezra and Nehemiah until the time of the Zugot,[84] the Torah was taught and interpreted to the citizens by the **scribes** (**Sofrim**) (cf. *Neh 8:3, 7-8*) – term that became synonymous with teachers, sages and scholars – and the Temple was ruled by the priests, in lack of a Judean monarchy. The students of the scribes were highly respected and known as Hassidim (pious ones).

• Alexander the Great conquered Israel (c. 330 BCE) and after his death his vast territory was divided by his officers. From these grew a wicked offshoot: Antioch Epiphanes (167 BCE) who wanted to eradicate Judaism and impose Hellenism by murdering every family that observed Torah and by desecrating the Holy Temple.[85] But Judah Maccabee,[86] son of Matityahu the priest, led a revolt against the Greeks that surprisingly succeeded, rejecting secularism and purifying the Temple. The dedication of the Temple is commemorated every year in the festival of Hannukah.[87]

• It was about this time that the period of the Zugot began, when the Hassidim Yose ben Yoezer and Yose ben Yohanan became the heads of the Sanhedrin and declared the impurity of the pagan nations (cf. *Shabbat 15a-b*).

• But the story does not end there. The world was still in war, and the Hellenes were yet over Israel, so Yonathan, brother of Judah Maccabee, in order to protect the Jews began to make diplomatic negotiations with the enemies; reason by which the ruler of the Seleucid kingdom (Alexander Balas; 150 BCE) made him the political leader and high-priest.[88] Sadly, his negotiations with the heathens became the cause of his death.[89] It was his successor and brother Shimon who gained the independence of Judea and purified Israel from secularism

---

[81] About 20 years before Common Era, the king Herod would remodel the Temple making it bigger.

[82] Cf. *Avot 1:1; Berakhot 33a; Megilah 2a, 17b.*

[83] Cf. *Bava Bathra 15a*. It was known as *"Torah, Prophets and Hagiographra" (B. b. 13b)*; or *"Torah, Prophets and Psalms" (Lk 24:22)*; acronym: *Tanakh*; alternatively: *Scripture (Miqra).*

[84] Zugot refers to a five generations period during the time of the Second Temple in which the Sanhedrin was overseen by a couple of rulers known as Nasi (president) and Av Beit-Din (vice-president of the court).

[85] cf. *1 Maccabees 1: 5-10, 37-39, 54-57; 3:1-3. Josephus "War of the Jews" 1:1-2.*

[86] cf. *1 Maccabees 3:1-3. Josephus, "Antiquities" 12:7.7.*

[87] cf. *Shabbat 21b; 2Mac 1:18+.*

[88] cf. *1 Maccabees 10:20.*

[89] cf. *Josephus "Antiquities" 13:5.10; 1Macabees 12: 46-49, 13:19.*

(143-142 BCE),[90] hence being chosen as the next High Priest and governor of Israel, pending the advent of a rightful prophet (Elijah or Messiah) (*1Mac. 14:41-42*). Here begins the Hasmonean period.

• The son of Shimon, Yohanan Hyrcanus, in a terrible mistake, decided to force by sword the conversion of the Idumeans; his descendants became thirsty of power, to the point of incarcerating their own family members and striving for the throne in civil wars; this caused the Roman empire to easily take the control of Israel (63 BCE). The Hasmonean bureaucracy was filled with men of Greek names, and the dynasty eventually became very Hellenized. Then, an Idumean descendant – Herod the Great – brought the Hasmonean dynasty to an end, having been proclaimed the new king of the Jews by the Roman senate[91] (37 BCE).
All the above reflects how the Jewish people were exposed to different philosophies and politics; thus causing a major diversity in schools of thought and political interests. Now we can dive into the 1st century.

(4.2) Geographical situation

1st Century Israel was divided into different provinces:

• In the North, near Syria (in the area that corresponds to the tribe of Naftali), we have **Galilee**, where Yeshua mostly lived and taught. Kefar-Nahum and Nazareth belong here.
• On the eastern side of the river there were gentile (and Roman controlled) areas: Caesarea of Philippi and the Decapolis; an area with ten cities (the land of the Gadarenes and Gergesenes).
• At the south of Galilee was **Samaria** (Ephraim and Menashe's area), where Yeshua healed ten lepers and visited Yaqov's well (*Gn 33:18-19*).
• At the south of Samaria was **Judea** (or Judah), where Roman domination and influence was way stronger. Its capital was Jerusalem; Yeshua went in pilgrimage here for the annual festivals and stayed at the end of his life for his ministry.

(4.3) The Pharisees

Apart from Hellenistic philosophers, Romans, Samaritans and many other individuals, there were three major Jewish movements:
(a) The Pharisees (b) the Sadducees (c) The Essenes.[92]

• The Pharisees (**Perushim**) apparently began as a 'separatist' party when the aristocracy of the priestly families began to rule arrogantly over Israel without taking into consideration the house of Judah, of whom it is written that: "legislator shall not depart from Judah, nor the lawgiver from between his feet" (cf. *Gn 49:10*). Unlike the Sadducees, they followed the traditions of the scribes (cf. *Berakhot 48b; 2Maccabees 14:3,37-38*).

• Two Pharisees: **Shammai and Hillel**, ended the Zugot era giving way to the Tannaim period. The only difference between the schools of Hillel and Shammai was in matters of legal law (known as hallakha), in which Hillel was generally more lenient and Shammai stricter; but in theology they were one and the same (i.e. Pharisees). They believed and taught the same traditions as they received them from the ancient scribes. Among them emerged the 'sages of Israel' (HaZaL).

[90] cf. *1 Maccabees 13:41; Josephus, "Antiq." 13: 6.6.*
[91] cf. *Josephus "Jewish wars", 1:14.4.*
[92] cf. *Antiquities 13:5.*

• By this time most **scribes (Sofrim)** were considered part of the School of Hillel.[93] In the New Testament they are involved in the trial of Paul, and after debating with the Sadducees they pleaded him not guilty (*Acts 23:9*). But let us not forget that there were also Herodian scribes – scribes that worked for Herod, and consequently for the Romans (*Matt. 2:4*).

• The New Testament speaks positively of two members of the School of Hillel: one of them **Gamaliel** (Hillel's grandson), a sage that is depicted as the Rabbi of Paul (*Acts 22:3*), and the one who defended the Nazarenes when they were in trouble (*Acts 5:34*). According to the Talmud he was a saint (tzaddiq) who observed with purity the Torah (*cf. Sotah 49a*) – and took Shammai's charge as head of the Pharisees.

• The second Pharisee that is depicted as a pious person, specifically in the Gospel of John, is **Nicodemus**, the Pharisee who came to learn from Yeshua, defended him in the false trial and also helped to bury him in the tomb of another rich Pharisee (*Jn 7:50-51, 19:40*). He very much fits the description of Naqdimon[94] --Nicodemus ben Gorion of Ruma, Galilee -- the wealthiest and most respected member of the peace party during the Jewish rebellion of 66, described as a saint.[95] A blur statement[96] in the Gemara might evidence that this Nicodemus was in fact a follower of Yeshua. A Baraita (*Sanhedrin 43a*) says that Yeshu had five disciples who were executed together: two of them named Naqai and Boni, and in the Gemara we are told that "Boni" was Nicodemus' original name (*Taanit 21a*).

• In the **Shammai** group there were sages of good heart, but (since Shammai was more conservative and stricter) some radicals used his school as a platform for their political agendas. Especially this is the case of the **Qanaim**[97] (ie. the **zealots**); a group that rose against anything that seemed to compromise Judaism – that is: hellenizers, Romans, intermixed marriages… etc) – one of Yeshua's disciple was called Shimon 'the Zealot' (*Lk 6:13*). Within the zealots there was a terrorist group called the sicarii (the assassins), and in one occasion they killed dozens of Hillel students in order to manipulate the votes to favor Shammai's decrees.[98] The historians say during Jerusalem's fall the Zealots' behaviour was crueller than the Romans'.

(4.4) The Sadducees

• The Sadducees **(Tzeduqim)** were considered heretics. They were (for the most part) rich people of the priestly family who degenerated into Hellenism and corrupted themselves with the Roman bribes. They were the "Sola-Scriptura" people of their time[99] with their own (materialistic) doctrines. Most rejected the resurrection of the dead, the immortality of the soul and many other things that (according to their own interpretation)[100] are not directly

---

[93] cf. *Rosh haShana 19a, Yerushalmi Berakhot 1:7.*

[94] cf. *Eiruvin 51b;* see Kefar Shikhin (Asochis) in *Josephus' Antiq. 13:337.*

[95] cf. *Josephus, "wars of the Jews" 2:20, 4:3, 9; cf. Levick B, Vespasian, 29-38; Taanit 21a, 19b; Gittin 56a.*

[96] prof. Yosef Klausner demonstrates (*in 'Yeshu miNatzeret'*) that this story is more an aggadah than an historical event, since the Baraita in Hebrew only says the name of the 5 disciples, whereas the other details that follow next are aggadic additions of the Amoraim in Aramaic. Besides, the later sages dealt with Yeshua and with a Yeshu contemporary of Rabbi Aqiva as if they were one, reason by which there are contradictions in the time periods, his parent's name, and the way he was executed (cf. *Sanh. 67a, 43a, Shabbat 44b. cf. Ariel Cohen Alloro's Yimakh Shmo*).

[97] While they are assumed to be Pharisees, Josephus and the Talmud count those in the later period as a fourth independent party (cf. *Antiq. 18:1.1, 6; Gittin 56b*).

[98] cf. *Shabbat 17a.*

[99] cf. *Josephus, "Antiq." 13:10.*

[100] cf. *Sanhedrin 90b; Josephus Refutatio 13:10.*

mentioned in the Written Torah. In fact, their interpretation of the Torah was so stringent and literal that the day their code was abolished Israel celebrated a festival (*Megilat Taanit 4*). The Pharisees had become so loved by the people that the Sadducees felt obliged to observe certain Pharisaic traditions as well.[101]

• The New Testament quite often refers the Sadducees as: 'the chief priests' – a term that remarks their aristocratic position. They are responsible for Yeshua's detention (*Matt. 26*). It is mentioned that the high priests in the false trial of Yeshua were the Sadducees **Annas and Qayapha** (*Jn 18:24*). Historians tell us that these two received their position by the Roman governor of Syria.[102] The sages talk about them as wicked and corrupt, who never wanted to abandon their position (*cf. Pesakhim 57a*) - reason by which a "King of the Jews" would be considered a threat. The book of Acts mentions the Sadducees working together with the Zealots to stop the Nazarene movement - in their case, because they felt offended with the doctrine of the 'resurrection of the dead' [the Nazarenes were claiming that their Rebbe had resurrected, and such a claim was threatening the credibility of the Sadducee's doctrines].[103] In fact, a great number of problems recorded in the book of Acts come from the Sadducees.

• **Paul of Tarsus** – a **Pharisee son of Pharisees** (*Acts 23:6*) – raised as a former disciple of Gamaliel in Jerusalem (*Acts 22:3*), had apparently embraced a zealot-like philosophy – working under the Sadducees supervision – to imprison the Nazarenes and to kill them if necessary (*Acts 8:1, 9:1, 9:13-14, 26:10; Gal 1:14*).

(4.5) The Essenes

• **The Essenes (Isiyim)** were, together with the Pharisees, another branch of Judaism that emerged from the original Hassidim. They, since the Hasmonean period, opposed the corruption in the Temple, and with the time formed separated communities in the desert. There were sub-groups among the Essenes too, but we do not know much of them because of their seclusion and because their texts are incomplete and cryptic. But we do know that some of them were famous for having divine revelations of the future, they expected the end of the pagan government, interpreted the Scriptures in an esoteric manner, most were vegetarians and many of their traditions and beliefs were very similar – if not identical – with that of the Pharisees, although their Hallakha (i.e. their way to walk in the Torah) was way more stringent. We also know that the House of Hillel was friendly with the Essenes. Before Shammai, the first 'pair mate' of Rabbi Hillel was Menahem the Essene.[104] Some scholars theorize that John the Baptist might have been part of an Essene community at some point, but we only have speculations.

In the Gospels (and N"T in general) there are religious expressions and ideas that for centuries have remained somehow obscure, but today they can be contextualized as they have been found in the Qumran scrolls, which are attributed to the Essenes.

---

[101] cf. *Sanh 33b*.

[102] cf. *Antiquites 20:9*.

[103] *Acts 4:1-2*.

[104] cf. *Hagiga 16b; Antiquities 15:10.5.* מנחם האיסיי

23

CHAPTER 5: Yeshua's Judaism

(5.1) to fulfil or to abolish?

Torah (a.k.a Pentateuch), has become in most Christian circles something opposed to God's will. They see the Torah as something that should be avoided, they claim it is legalist, prehistoric, unnecessary... and they refer to it with the derogatory name of **"the Law"** [105] as something opposed to 'God's Grace'. They claim that Yeshua annulled it and replaced it with pure Grace. This predominant view is summed up in the words of the 5th century Christian philosopher Socrates Scholasticus:

> "When Judaism was changed into Christianity,
> the obligation to observe the Mosaic law and the ceremonial types ceased". [106]

The claim does not make it true, though. This approach makes any reconciliation with Judaism impossible. What, then, was Yeshua's real relationship with the Torah?

• **Yeshua was raised in an orthodox Jewish family** and was **circumcised** on the eighth day. His parents were observant Jews who did everything according to the Torah of Moses (*Lk 2:22-24, 27*) and celebrated the Jewish holidays in Jerusalem every year (*Lk 2:41-42*). Yeshua went on pilgrimage as well, even for lesser and post-biblical festivals, such as Hannuka (*Jn 5:1, 10:22*).

He said to a Samaritan[107] that salvation is of the Jews (*Jn 4:22*). He taught from Torah and his disciples called him Rabbi (meaning 'teacher'; a pharisaic title). He was, therefore, a good observant Jew. Did he change later?

• Do the Gospels depict a Yeshua that has the intention to reject, annul, or replace the Torah of Moses with something else?[108] If we ask him what would he answer?

> "Do not even think that I came to abolish the Torah or the Prophets.
> I did not come to abolish but to fulfil" (*Matt. 5:17*).

He says that the mere idea should not even pass through our mind. It must be noticed that "fulfil" refers to obedience, [109] to fully obey and to cause others to obey. Fulfilling is the very opposite of 'abolishing'. Rabbi Yonathan taught: "whoever fulfils the Torah in poverty, his end will be fulfil it in wealth" [i.e., he will be rewarded for his obedience] (*Avot 4:9*).

• Yeshua believed that **each single Hebrew letter** of the Torah was meaningful. "It is easier for Heaven and Earth to pass than one apex of the Torah to fail" (*Lk 16:17*). "In no way one Yod

---

[105] Josephus demonstrates that Greek-speaking Jews expanded the meaning the word "*nomos*" (Law) as to refer the Torah. Josephus defines it as 'theocracy': not only including laws against sin, but also ethical morals, universal love of humans, perseverance, and piety (cf. *contra Apion 1:8, 2:15, 17*).

[106] *Socrates Scholasticus; book 5:22.*

[107] Samaritans (*Shamerim*) are probably a hybrid of Ephraimites, Menashites and pagans brought to Samaria in the Assyrian deportation (*2Kings 17; 2Chr 34:9*); they worship in mount Gezirim instead of Jerusalem and their Torah differs with the Jewish one on the worship place chosen by God.

[108] For centuries Judaism has believed this based on Rambam's words: "he [Yeshua the Christian] caused Israel to be killed by the sword, their remnants to be dispersed and humiliated, the Torah to be switched for something else, and most of the world to worship a god other than the God of Israel" (*Hilkhot Melakhim 11:4*). There are two possibilities: *(a)* Rambam refers to the Christian Jesus (Yeshua as he is perceived by Christians and as was misused by the Catholic Inquisition) *(b)* Or Rambam learnt this by Christians and never read the Gospels himself. An unbiased reading of the Gospels shows a completely different scenery from what Rambam describes.

[109] Despite the Christendom's attempt to give it a different meaning.

(ʼ) or one apex from the Torah pass until all be fulfilled" (*Matt. 5:18*). Notice that the Heaven and Earth passing away is a reference to the end times in Isaiah 51:6, which has not happened yet.

• He commanded his disciples **to adhere** to the Torah of Moses.[110] He said: 'Whoever breaks one of these little commandments [of the Torah] and teach men to do so, he will be called the least in the kingdom of Heaven, but whoever does and teaches the same will be called great in the Kingdom of Heaven' (*Matt 5:19*). Our sages taught in the same manner: "Whoever thinks that the Torah is Heavenly except for one verse, because they think that verse was added by Moses, of that person it is written (*Nm 15:31*): he has despised the word of the Lord" (*Sanhedrin 99a*).

• **Yeshua's love for the Torah** is especially notorious when he is directly asked what the greatest commandment is. He responded with the '**Shema**' (*Mark 12:28-31*) "Hear Israel, the Lord is your God, the Lord is One, and you must love the Lord…etc" (*Deut 6:4*). Considered the heart of Judaism, it is recited twice per day by all Jews from the moment they are able to speak until their very death. It defines the perfect monotheistic creed of Judaism and the acceptance of the yoke of the kingdom of Heaven.

Another command is equally important: "Love your neighbor as yourself", as it was taught in the school of Rabbi Hillel, "This is the greatest principle of the Torah".[111] Once a gentile asked Rabbi Hillel to teach him the essence of the Torah; he answered with one single principle: "What is hateful to you, do not to your fellow man. This is the entire Torah; the rest is the commentary. Go and study it" (*Shabbat 31a*). In the same manner Yeshua taught: "In everything, you do to others what you would have them to do to you, for this sums up the Torah and the Prophets" (*Matt 7:12*). The similarity of phraseology is not a mere coincidence.[112]

(5.2) The 'You have heard... but I say' Antithesis

After saying: "I did not come to abolish but to fulfil", the next thing Yeshua does is teaching what we call the 'Antithesis of the Sermon of the Mount', which consists in extracting Mussar – i.e. moral principles – from the Torah (*Matt 5-6*). In some cases here, Yeshua imposes 'fences' on the commandments, based on the moral principles and ethics inherent in the Torah (which are called 'mussar'). Because of the formula: "**You have heard… but I say**", some believe that Yeshua is attacking the interpretation of the sages (others say: interpretation of men); so "You have heard" refers to the sages of Israel, and "But I say" is a divine revelation that corrects the sages. Others believe that this is a radical new interpretation of the Bible (never seen before in Judaism); in other words: "You have heard" is the 'Law', and "But I say" is the New Covenant that replaces and/or overtakes the Law. Both approaches are mistaken. Let us see the truth of this:

---

[110] Yaqov Emden (a great authority in Judaism), after quoting Matthew chapter 5, says: 'It is therefore exceedingly clear that the Nazarene never dreamed of destroying the Torah'. A few paragraphs before, he had quoted Paul (*Gal 5:3*) and claimed that even according to Paul the circumcised ones are still bound to obey the entire Torah (cf. *Emden, Seder Olam Rabba vezuta*).

[111] *sifra, kedoshim 4:12 [89b]; Bereshit Rabbah 24:7.*

[112] It is worth noticing that, although in Matthew's account the scribe who asks about the greatest command is depicted as someone testing Yeshua, Mark's account actually describes a friendly attitude and both Yeshua and the scribe praise each other for their words at the end (*Mark 12:28-34*).

(a) 'But I say' has its parallel in the Qumran texts,[113] where the rules of different schools are juxtaposed with the expression 'But we say' (אנחנו אומרים).

(b) Nothing of what Yeshua said in the sermon of the Mount was 'new'. Rather, everything he said is word by word Pharisaic theology, and that cannot be a mere coincidence.

So, let us analyze the Antithesis in the Sermon of the Mount.

(5.3) You shall not murder (Mt 5:21)

Yeshua teaches that one is not only guilty of murder for literally killing someone, but also for insulting and enraging against his brother, and such person deserves punishment either by the Sanhedrin or by the fire of Gehenna (5:22-25).[114]

The statement does not contradict the Torah, since it is based on its ethical principles (cf. Lv 19:17). Similarly, the sages taught: 'he who embarrasses his neighbor openly, it is as if he spilled blood' (Bava Metzia 58b) and also: "An evil eye... and hatred of men put one out of the world" (Avot 2:16).

(5.4) Do not commit Adultery (Mt 5:27)

Yeshua says that adultery can be committed by lusting after a woman. In this very context he adds that the eye and the right hand can be instruments of sin and it is better to cut them off than to go to hell with the full body (Mt 5:27-30).

Equally the sages taught: 'Adultery can be committed with the eyes' (Vayikra Rabbah 23), and "A man must not have sexual thoughts during the day, so that he would not become unclean wasting his seed at night" (Avodah Zara 20b). As a matter of fact, the Mishna uses a strong and hyperbolic language by saying that the hand of a [Jewish] man that frequently touches his genitals should be chopped off (cf. Nidda 13a), and also: "it is preferable for the belly to be split than going down to the pit of destruction" (Nidda 13b).

(5.5) the certificate of divorce (Mt 5:31)

He taught that the valid reason for divorcement is fornication and otherwise the couple is still considered married (Matt 5:31-32).

This interpretation is based on a Hebrew word in the Torah: "If a man... has found _Ervah_ [in his wife], he must write for her a letter of divorcement" (Deut 24:1). What does 'Ervah' mean?

Ervah means nudity or pudenda, but it can also mean shame or disgrace. Uncovering the Ervah of a woman is an idiom for 'cohabiting' with her (Lv 18:6).

It is from this word that the school of Shammai ruled that "a man should not divorce his wife unless he has found some unseemly thing", while the school of Hillel interpreted that any reason that causes disgrace or shame to her husband can be a reason of divorcement (Mishna Gittin 90a).

This debate took place during Yeshua's lifetime, and he clearly took a side.[115] This is one of the few times, if not the only one, where Yeshua appears to side with the school of Shammai[116]

---

[113] cf. 4QMMT B55, 65, 68, 73.

[114] 'Fire of Gehenna' is 'the anger of God' (cf. Is 66:16, 24). Gehenna is the Rabbinic name of the place where the imperfect soul gets purged after death (Pesakhim 54a). There are seven levels of purification, depending the status of each soul (Sotah 10b). If a soul cannot be purged, it falls in the state of Avadon (destruction) (Zohar I:62b Noah; cf. Eiruvin 19a; Pesakhim 118a; Shabbat 33b; Bava Metzia 58b). The 'fire of Gehenna' refers to judgment in this world as well, which is shown in the Great Flood and in Sodom (Midrash Eduyot 2:10; Jud 1:7).

[115] It must not be understood as an isolated absolute law; there are other sceneries where divorcement is permitted and/or necessary (cf. Ex 21:11). But that is beyond the scope of this essay.

[116] 'School of Shammai' does not equal Shammai himself, and neither 'school of Hillel' is Hillel himself.

instead of Hillel's. Of course, this was for Hassidut's sake: he chose the most ideal principle for the members of the messianic kingdom, where our righteousness must go beyond what is legally allowed or forbidden.

(5.6) Do not break your oath (Mt 5:33)

The Torah allows to swear, in fact it is one of the requirements in the investigation of an adulterous woman (*Nm 5:19*), but the words of an oath are not taken lightly by God (*cf. Lv 5:4*). It specifically commands not to swear falsely by God's Name (*Lv 19:12*).
Yeshua taught not to swear at all, but rather "let your yes be yes and your no be no". Because even if you do not swear in the name of God directly, God is included in every oath, and it is a grave sin not to keep an oath (*Matt 5:33-37*). Our sages of blessed memory raised a fence on the command by saying: "Do not swear at all, not even if it is true" (*Tanhuma Vayikra*). They also taught: "the characteristic of a righteous person is that his yes is yes and his no is no" (*Bava Bathra 49b*).

(5.7) An Eye for an Eye (Mt 5:38)

Keeping in mind that Shammai outlived Hillel and probably his school was more influential than that of Hillel in Yeshua's days, maybe <u>some</u> Shammaite Pharisees (as well as Sadducees and probably Samaritans) applied literally the command 'an eye for an eye' (*Ex 21:24; Lv 24:19*). However, most Pharisaic schools interpreted this verse differently,[117] among other things, because the Torah does not allow personal revenge (*Deut 19:16-21; Prov 20:22; 24:29*), so the 'eye for an eye' command only makes sense in the context of Jewish judicial courts.
To better express the idea that the command does not allow personal vendettas, Yeshua paraphrases the words of the prophet: "Let him offer his cheek to the one that strike him" (*Lam 3:30*). Yeshua's teaching, "do not resist an evil person" is also a Pharisaic teaching (*Yoma 23a*) which is beautifully reflected in the words of Rebbe Nahman of Breslev, who said: "The true sign of a person who has returned to God is the ability to hear himself insulted and remain silent... Repentance essentially depends on humility. One must make oneself into nothing... pay no attention whatsoever to opposition or abuse from others" (*Likutei Moharan I, 6*).
In addition to this, the Torah teaches: "If you see your foe's donkey lying under its load... you shall help him to release it" (*Ex 23:5*). "Hillel said: Be among the disciples of Aaron, loving peace and pursuing peace, loving creatures and bringing them closer to the Torah" (*Avot 1:12*), as it is similarly stated in Scripture: "If your enemy is hungry give him bread" (*Prov 25:21*).

(5.8) Love your Neighbour, hate the enemy (Mt 5:43)

"Hate your enemy" does not appear in the Torah; it is not a Torah commandment. Rather, it was an opinion raised in several circles. For instance, hating the children of darkness was one of the laws of the Essenes. Also, (although it is not the case) one might think of this rabbinical account: Rabbi Nahman bar Yitzhak was expounding on the verse "If you see your foe's donkey..." (*Ex 23:5*), and making use of Proverbs[118] (*8:13*) inferred that "it is a duty to hate [a Jewish person that transgresses the Torah and is found in indecency]" (*Pesakhim 113b*).
Yet, commentators are careful to explain that in this case 'hate' refers not to the feeling of hatred, but to a rejection and separation in order to cause the sinner to repent.[119] Ibn Ezra

---

[117] The Pharisees understood that 'an eye for an eye' (עין תחת עין) can be paid with an equivalent monetary compensation of the harm done (*Bava Kama 83b-84a*); in cases of conspiracy, with lashes (*Makot 1:1*). In the Talmud the argument of each school is challenged by... other Pharisees?
[118] "God's commandment is to hate wickedness" (*Prov 8:13*).
[119] cf. *Rashi on Arakhin 16b. Rambam on Hilkhot Rotzeiakh 13:14.*

stresses that in the Exodus verse, the literal meaning is 'one who hates you' and not 'one whom you hate'.[120]

Concerning the Psalms of David where he says he hates God's enemies, it must be noticed that he says this from a nationalist point of view, in the context of wars and his own persecutions and not in the context of personal relationships. In fact, one of the most notorious characteristics of King David was precisely his love for his enemies (2S 1:17, 19:4, 6), so Rabbi Nahman of Breslev taught that "when reciting Psalms one should imagine that King David's battles are one's own personal battles against his Evil Tendency" (Likutei Moharan II:125).

In short, what does Yeshua say? He teaches, "Love your enemies and pray for those who persecute you" (Matt 5:44-48).[121] The Talmud gives a similar point of view:

> "There were once some thugs in Rabbi Meir's neighborhood who caused him a great deal of trouble. Rabbi Meir therefore prayed that they should die. His wife Beruria said to him: What, do you think that it is written: Let sinners cease? (Psal 104:35) Is it really written sinners? It is written 'sins'! (Khataim!) Further, look at the end of the verse: 'And then the wicked will be no more.' Once the sins cease, then the wicked will be no more! Rather pray for them that they should repent, and the wicked will be no more. He did pray for them, and they repented". (Berakhot 10a)

Mar Zutra used to pray when climbed into his bed: "I forgive those who have vexed me" (Megillah 28a). After all, "If you hate any man, you hate God who made man in his image" (Midrash Tanhuma).

(5.9) To be seen by men (Mt 6:1)

In the next three paragraphs Yeshua talks about Charity (6:1), Prayer (6:5) and Fasting (6:16). He insists that none of the three things must be done "to be seen by men". He is talking about the intention of the heart – what in Judaism we call kavanah.[122] Giving charity or praying or fasting without proper kavanah is not meritorious.

Our sages similarly taught that giving charity without the beggar knowing from whom he receives, delivers a man from unnatural death (Bava Bathra 10a-b). And about prayer: "He who prays loudly in order to be heard is a person of little faith" (Berakhot 24b).

Yeshua also taught that extending the prayer does not make it better. Our sages taught in the same manner: "If one extends his prayer expecting fulfilment in the end will receive vexation of heart" (Berakhot 55a). He added: "because your Father knows what you need even before you ask for it" (Matt 6:8). Our sages taught as well: 'God knows our thoughts before they were formed' (Bereshit Rabbah 9).

(5.10) The Avinu

Yeshua concludes the prayer section by teaching the "**Our Father**" (Avinu); the most famous prayer ever, also known as 'the lord's prayer'. Although it might be totally new, the truth is that its content resembles very much (with its variations) the 3rd, 5th, 6th, 9th and 15th blessings

---

[120] See the same idea depicted in Matthew 18: 14-17.

[121] Here it must be noticed that he refers to personal and individual relationships in the highest level of piety (Hassidut) which will be the standard in the Messianic era. In no way this annuls the Torah principles of defending one's own life if required, or defending someone else, or even your country in a national level; because Torah never commands to encourage passively the wickedness of the wicked. Sadly, most people cannot conceive the harmonization of these two seemingly paradoxical principles.

[122] See the Rif (on Rosh haShana 28) where he quotes the Gemara (114a) to prove that the Hallakha goes according to those who ruled that it is required to have a proper intention when performing commandments (also Raavad on the Rif and Ramban in Milkhamot HaShem).

of a prayer established by the Great Assembly, known as the Amidah (I am not claiming it is the Amidah, which is not, but the similarity of content is notorious). The ambiguous phrase: "forgive our faults as we forgive our debtors" has its parallel in ancient Jewish books: "forgive the hurt done by your neighbour and you'll be forgiven when you pray" (*Sirakh 28:2*).[123]

The community of disciples established that the Avinu should be prayer three times per day (cf. *Didache 8:3*), which implies it goes together with the Amidah. Yeshua was not the only Rebbe to teach his disciples his own prayer: John the Baptist also taught his disciples a personal prayer (*Lk 11:1-2*). In fact, there were so many sages who would compose a personalized supplemental prayer for his students, which they would attach at the end of the Amidah (cf. *Berakhot 16b-17a*). This way, each school was distinguished by their master's prayer. For example,

> "Upon concluding his prayer Rabbi Yohanan would say: May it be your will, Adonai our God, that you look upon our shame and behold our evil. Then dress yourself in mercy, cover yourself with strength, wrap yourself in kindness and gird yourself in grace. May the attribute of goodness and gentleness come before you".

Mar bar Hanina composed the following prayer for the Amidah:

> "My God, guard my tongue from evil and my lips from speaking deceit. To those who insult me may my soul be silent. May my soul be like dust to everyone. Open my heart to your Torah so that my soul will look for your commandments. Deliver me from harm, from evil inclination, evil women, and all evil that occurs in this world. As for those who think evil of me, speedily annul their counsel and frustrate their plans. May the words of my mouth and the meditation of my heart be acceptable before you, Adonai, my rock and my redeemer".

Other Rebbes such as Shelah haKadosh (Horovitz), Rabbi Isaac Luria or Rebbe Nahman of Breslev also composed prayers that their followers would include in their list of daily prayers.

I could go on drawing parallels between the Sermon of the Mount and Jewish literature, such as: "do not store for yourselves treasures on earth" (*Matt 6:19*) which is found in Bava Bathra (*11a*), but enough to say that having reviewed the Antithesis portion I have found nothing that contradicts the Torah or the sages of Israel. On the contrary, I have found that Yeshua happens to reflect word by word the teachings of the Pharisees. And the hints that Yeshua himself might have been a Pharisee do not end here.

---

[123] *See also "Yalkut Vayikra" 613.*

CHAPTER 6: Orthodox Observance

(6.1) He wore Tzitzit

Orthodox observance is a modern expression, used to address those who follow or observed the Torah according to the traditional mainstream Judaism. Yeshua's Judaism was not limited to moral values; he was an "orthodox" in every sense of the word, and his disciples were trained under the very same standards. Some Christians are of the opinion that Yeshua did not abolish the Torah, but that his disciples did it a few years later. If they did, then they did not follow their master, did they?

Yeshua wore tzitzit. We all have heard the story of a diseased woman with a permanent issue of blood who came near Yeshua and was healed by touching the "hem of his garment" (*Matt 9:20*), and also many other sufferers who were healed by touching Yeshua's "hem" (*Matt 14:36*).
A Jew reading this portion automatically knows what the text is saying, but for a gentile the meaning is lost in the translation. Torah commands Jews to wear fringes in their four corner garments in order to bring to memory all the commandments of God and prevent them from doing something immoral in their daily routines.[124] The fringes in Hebrew are called: **tzitziot**, or simply tzitzit.
Originally tzitziot were dyed with a specific blue dye called: **tekhelet**. This became another name for the fringes and, incidentally, it appears in the Aramaic manuscripts of the N"T.[125]
Every observant Jew wore tassels or tzitzit; Yeshua was not an exception. But he was of the opinion that one should not enlarge the tzitzit in order to be noticed by others, which he considered hypocrisy (*Matt 23:5*).
The prophecy in Zechariah says that in the future ten men out of every nation and tongue will hold the border of the garment of each Jew and say: we want to go with you (*Zech 8:23*). It is therefore assumed in the prophecy that Jews will still wear tzitzit in the future. And no, nowhere in the Gospels or in the N"T Yeshua abolished this command.

(6.2) He wore Tefillin

When Yeshua attacks the hypocrisy of those who lengthen their tzitzit in order to be noticed, he includes in that statement those who make board their "**phylacteries**" (*Matt 23:5*).
What are the "**phylacteries**"? They are two small boxes which contain a scroll of the Shema prayer and are put on the forehead and on the arm, tied with a leather strap. Archaeologists discovered ancient boxes from many different sects that also included the Decalogue, and priestly ones which contained the priestly blessing.
Their real name is "**tefillin**". Now "phylacteries" (amulets) is an unfortunate translation because the tefillin were NOT amulets, and there is no historical record that they were at any time used as such. "Tefillin" is the plural of tefillah, which means prayer – because (**1st**) the boxes contain a prayer and (**2nd**) because they are worn during prayer.
The story of the tefillin goes back to the Torah itself, to the Shema prayer itself:

"These words [i.e., the Shema]... you shall bind them as a sign (לאות, symbol, mark) on your hand and they shall be as frontlets between your eyes" (לטטפת, *Dt 6:8*). Other portion says: "as a memorial (לזכרון, i.e. something that makes you remember) between your eyes" (*Ex 13:9*). I

---

[124] *Nm 15:38-39; Dt 22:12;* cf. *Menahot 41a*
[125] "They lengthen their tekhelet" - "ומורכין תכלתא" (*Matt 23:5 in the Peshitta*).

understand that those who have never had contact with Judaism might believe that Yeshua was against tefillin, but if we look closer to the text, we will find the opposite:

(a) Yeshua does not criticize people who wear tefillin; what he criticizes is the hypocrisy of those who make them bigger in order to be noticed in public.

(b) Yeshua includes in the same critic "those who enlarge their tassels", and as we have seen, Yeshua himself wore tassels, so he cannot be against the use of tassels and phylacteries. Instead, he is against a hypocritical use of them.

(c) In the context in which Yeshua says this, he is commanding his disciples to obey the Pharisees and the scribes. All together implies that Yeshua and his disciples wore tefillin too, but in modesty. It is similar to the Sermon of the Mount, when he commands his followers not to pray loudly in order to be noticed by others.

Even the Christian Justin Martyr in his dialogue with Trypho affirms that Deuteronomy 6:8 commands to wear "phylacteries" and he defines them as "Holy" (cf. *Dial. 46*).

(6.3) He encouraged Temple sacrifices

Yeshua was passionate about the Temple. As we have seen, he made pilgrimage to Jerusalem for every Jewish festival and went to the Temple, where he taught (*Mr 14:49*). His disciples apply to him the verse: "the zeal of your House consumes me" (*Psal 69:10 [9]; cf. Jn 2:17*). When Yeshua foresaw the destruction of Jerusalem and the Temple, he lamented on it (*Lk 19:41, 46*). He loved the Temple and what the Temple represents.

He healed ten lepers (*Lk 17:12-13*) telling them to go to the high priest as established in the Torah, and as per the Torah, the cleansing of leprosy includes the offering of sacrifices in the Temple (*Lv 14:2*). Yeshua was perfectly aware of this and never censored the offerings in the altar (*Matt 5:24*).

Did he abolish the Levitical service after his death? Many years after Yeshua's passing away his students were still a temple community (*Lk 24:53*), who entered the Temple every day for the worship times [with their respective daily sacrifices].[126] Even more! Keifa and the other disciples from Galilee moved to live in Jerusalem in order to be in the Temple.

It is true, though, that some groups accused Paul of going against the Temple. But he defended himself and said he did not do anything against the Torah or the Temple (*Acts 25:8*), and that the people who accused him have no proof of their accusations (*Acts 24:13-14*). In fact, to prove he did not cease his Torah observance, he did a nazarite vow for him and others (*Acts 18:18, 21:24*) and such a vow requires sacrifices in the Temple (*Nm 6:2-18*), which he offered (*Acts 24:17*). The event gives us two choices: Or Paul was honest in his claim that he was not against Torah observance, or he was a complete hypocrite, but this essay is not about Paul.

The prophets imply that the Temple will be reestablished for the Messianic era and sacrifices will be reinstated - at least for a while (*Zech 8:3; Ez 37:26-27; Is 2:2-3*). It is clearly stated that "I will make a righteous branch sprout from David [i.e Messiah]... because David will never fail to have a man to sit on the throne of the house of Israel, nor will the Levitical priests ever fail to have a man to... continually offer burnt-offerings, to burn grain-offerings and to present sacrifices" (*Jer 33:15-18*). Our sages explain that at some moment in the Messianic era, when the generation is ready and does not want to offer animals anymore, the priests will be solely dedicated to grain-offerings, as it is written: "And the grain-offering will be acceptable to HaShem" (*Mal 3:4*). (cf. *Tanhuma Emor 19, Vayikra Rabbah 9:7; Arakhin 21a; cf. Olat Reiyah vol. I, p. 292*)

---

[126] *Acts 2:46, 3:1, 5:21, 24:18; cf. Psa 55:18 [17]; Dan 6:11; Mishna Berakhot 4:1; Berakhot 26b.*

CHAPTER 7: The Oral Torah

(7.1) He was not Sola-Scriptura

One of the most notorious reforms among those of the Protestant movement was the inclusion of Karaism (or Sola-Scriptura). The Gospels... in fact the entire N"T is filled with Jewish oral traditions. If there is something we know for certain, is that Yeshua and his disciples were not Karaites – they did not go by canonical Scripture alone. They followed Oral Tradition in both senses: **(1)** Jewish legend: Aggadah. **(2)** and Jewish Law of behavior: Hallakha.

It should be noted in this essay that there is a tendency among present-day Jews to judge Yeshua in light of our modern Hallakha. That should not be the case considering (and scholars agree on this) [127] that our current Hallakha does not apply to the mid 1st century. Much of the Rabbinic Hallakha was developed between the 2nd and 5th centuries. 1st century Judaism was not a monolithic religion (if has ever been). We have already mentioned that even among the Pharisees there was disagreement concerning Jewish Law, and there were differences between Judean and Galilean observance as well. Nevertheless, there is a pattern in the Gospels that pretty much reflects the Hallakha of that time.

(7.2) Hallakha

• **On Baptism**. If you were a Sola-Scriptura Jew and you met for the first time 'John the Baptist' [128] **baptizing other Jews for the remission of their sins** (*Mark 1:4*) – you would literally freak out. The Torah does not say anywhere that I have to immerse in water as part of my repentance! That is NOWHERE found. Yet, the first thing Yeshua did in his ministry was **to get baptized by John the Baptist** (*Matt 3:13*). Later he commanded his disciples to do the same with every new disciple and every new convert (*Matt 28:19; Acts 8:38*).

The question is: why? Most Christian circles believe that John the Baptist invented the doctrine of baptism by divine command, but that is simply not true. The answer is that the Pharisees and Essenes immersed in water to **(1)** the new converts and **(2)** those who had been defiled in some way. They taught: "[the proselytes] shall enter the covenant [of Judaism] only by circumcision, baptism and [in the time of the Temple] with a sacrifice" (*Kritot 9a*). Also: "On good days a person may be baptized to become pure" (*Shulkhan Arukh 511:3; cf. Beitza 18*).

• **Yeshua recited blessings before meals** (*Matt 14:19, Mr 8:7, 14:22*), but the Torah only commands to pray grace AFTER meals – not before (*Dt 8:10*). However, our sages taught that "a man is forbidden to taste anything before saying a blessing over it" (*Berakhot 35a*). In addition, he always **broke the bread** after the blessing and shared it with his people (*Mr 8:6; Matt 26:26; Lk 24:30*). His disciples did this as well (*Acts 2:42, 20:7, 27:33-35*) because it is a common Jewish practice that the host who makes the blessing over the bread will also break it and give it to the others, as our sages say: "the guests may not eat anything until the one who breaks the bread has tasted it" (*Berakhot 47a*), and also: "the one who acts as a host may not break the bread until the guests have finished responding Amen [to the haMotzi prayer (which is the blessing over bread)]" (*ibid*). Pharisees and Essenes followed this tradition and so Yeshua did too.

---

[127] "What we're seeing more and more through the research and the archaeological discoveries is how diverse Judaism was in this period" (Michael White *"from Jesus to Christ"* part I).

[128] Or 'John the Immerser' – 'Yohanan haMatbil' – יוחנן המטביל. Ar. Yuhanon Ma'amdana – יוחנן מעמדנא

• He said **it is not appropriate to fast in the presence of the bridegroom** (*Matt 9:15*).[129] Although he is speaking allegorically, this idea comes, not from the Bible, but from our sages, who taught: "A bridegroom and his friends are free from the obligation of the Sukka [during the feast of tabernacles]... because they have to rejoice... and there is no real rejoicing except where the banquet is held" (*Sukka 25b*).

• **During the Passover** meal it is written that Yeshua "**sat reclined** together with the twelve" (*Matt 26:20*). [some Bibles render it as "sat", but the original says: "reclined"]. Why did he "recline" to eat the Passover? Because our sages established: "Even the poorest man in Israel must not eat [the Passover meal] until he reclines" (*Pesakhim 99b [Mishna 10:1]*).

• **During the Passover** meal it is also written that he "**took THE cup of wine**" (*Matt 26:27*), as if we already knew which specific cup of wine the text is referring to. It is because our sages established that "a man... should be given no less than four cups of wine [on Passover night, representing the four redemptions of Israel]" (*Pesakhim 99b [Mishna 10:1]*).

• After the Passover meal **they sang a hymn** (*Mark 14:26*). It is customary and even decreed to accompany the Passover meal with praising songs such as the Hallel (praise).[130] Additional songs are sung after the meal (in this case the hymn varies depending on the local custom of each community).
Notice that in this Passover meal Yeshua tells his disciples that he is going to be betrayed, arrested and executed, a topic that might have been brought as a revelation (pesher) or simply derived from the imagery depicted in some portions of the Hallel song.[131]

• It is noteworthy that throughout the entire New Testament the **Sacred Name is not pronounced not even once**. Instead, it is replaced with circumlocutions such as: Heaven, Father, God, the Lord.. etc. The reason the Name does not appear is not some kind of hidden plot to erase God's name (as the Sacred Namers claim) – That would make no sense considering there is not even ONE manuscript (out of more than 5000) with the Sacred Name on it. The reason is that the sages of the Great Assembly (4th Century BCE) imposed a gezeirah (i.e. a fence) during the exile, based on the command: "Do not pronounce the Name of the Lord your God unnecessarily" (*Ex 20:7*; cf. *Avodah Zara 18a*). In Judaism and in Jewish books the exact very same thing is done: when reading the Torah, they say Adonai (the Lord) instead of the Sacred Name, but even in the later books of the Hebrew Bible (Esther, Daniel, Ecclesiastes) the Name tends to be avoided already. Therefore, if Yeshua and his followers adhered to this fence, I suggest you do the same.

The **Gezeirot** (*cf. Yevamot 21a*) are fences around a command, built by the Rabbis, in order not to violate the actual command. Their use is deduced from verses such as: "Protect my statutes and my judgments" (*Lv 28:16*).

• Yeshua used **Pharisaic methods of Biblical interpretation**. Especially – but not only – the seven rules of Hillel.[132] These are seven methods of hermeneutics that (despite the name) are considered part of the Oral Torah given to Moses at Sinai.

---

[129] cf. *Thomas #104*.

[130] cf. *Pesakhim 95a [Mishna]*. Hallel is a verbatim recitation of the Psalms 113-118.

[131] "The anguish of the grave came upon me; I was overcome by trouble and sorrow. Then I called on the name of HaShem: O HaShem, save me... For you, HaShem, have delivered my soul from death, my eyes from tears, my feet from stumbling that I may walk before HaShem in the land of the living... Precious in the sight of HaShem is the death of his saints" (*Psalm 116:3-15*).

[132] cf. *Avot D'Rabbi Nathan 37*; cf. *Samson of Chinon, "sefer haKritot"*.

Yeshua uses them all, but especially the first one called: **Kal vaKhomer**.

Kal vaKhomer (lit. light and weighty) is a method of exegesis that states: "what is exceptionally true on small cases, must apply in more serious cases too". It can be inferred from Moses' words: "If you have been rebellious while I am still alive, how much more after my death?" (*Dt 31:27*), so the Kal vaKhomer arguments always use the same tagline: "If this is so… how much more….etc". Yeshua and Paul constantly use this method of exegesis. "If wicked humans give good gifts to their children, how much more the Heavenly Father… etc" (*Lk 11:13*). "If God clothes the grass… how much more will he clothe you?" (*Lk 12:28*). "If you were grafted into a cultivated olive tree, how much more readily will these, the natural branches be grafted into their own olive tree?" (*Rom 11:24*).

• As stated, he uses many other Jewish methods such as midrash (or pesher), or the so called 32 rules of Aggadic exegesis of Eliezer bar Yosi the Galilean.[133] Through these methods one can see the underlying reason for his continuous use of parables and non-verbatim paraphrased Scriptural verses (*cf. Jn 6:31, 19:37; Rom 11:26-27; 1Co 15:45*).[134] For instance, Yeshua's famous saying: "Whosoever exalts himself will be humbled, and whosoever humbles himself will be exalted" (*Lk 14:11*) is a paraphrase of Psalm 113, verses 5b & 6a.[135] The Midrash quotes this Psalm in the exact same manner in the mouth of Rabbi Hillel, as a proof-verse of his saying: "my self-abasement is my exaltation, and my self-exaltation is my abasement" (*Vayikra Rabbah 1:5*).

(7.3) Theology

• Yeshua is depicted as performing miracles in a daily manner, similar to those of the prophet Elisha (*2K 4:4-7, 20-36, 42-44, 5:14, 13:20-21*). He uses these **healing miracles as proof that the Kingdom of Heaven is among us and redemption is at hand** (*Matt 11:4-5; Lk 4:18; 11:20; Jn 10:38; Acts 2:22*). The miracles happened because of people's faith or worthiness as we are told there were places where Yeshua could not perform them (*Mr 6:5*). We do not necessarily identify Messiah by his capacity to perform miracles because (a) Bar Kokhva was a potential Messiah yet he did not perform any miracle, and (b) wizards and false prophets also perform miracles.[136] Some sages, such as Pinkhas ben Yair, Nahum of Gamzu, Honi and R. Hanina performed miracles (*Hulin 7a; Taanit 21a, 23a, 25a*), and Yeshua's disciples performed miracles as well (*Mr 16:20*). So obviously, miracles do not show per se that he who performs them is the Messiah, but according to Rambam Messiah will surely perform wonders and silence kings (*Iggeret Teiman XVII*). Our sages have this saying: "As it was with the first redeemer so will it be with the last redeemer" (*Bamidbar Rabbah 11:3*), and we know that Moses offered three signs to Israel to prove he had been sent by God (cf. *Ex 4:2*).

Rabbi Abraham ben David (Rambam's commentator) argued that there is a tradition in which Bar Kokhva was put to death by the sages themselves when he failed to produce the signs of Messiah, the example being Messiah's faculty to judge by the smell (cf. *Sanh 93b*), as it is written: "And he will smell with the fear of HaShem" (*Is 11:3*). On the 1st century the Psalm 146 was interpreted as testifying that the Kingdom of God (or the Messianic redemption) is accompanied with "sight to the blind" "justice for the oppressed"… etc. The last verse says:

---

[133] cf. *Rashi on Gen 2:8 & Horayot 3b; Samson of Chinon "Sefer Keritot"*.

[134] e.g. Rabeinu Tam uses these methods when he paraphrases Isaiah 2:3 to apply it to the Italian Rabbinate "For from Bari shall come forth Torah, and the word of the Lord from Tàranto" (*Sefer haYashar, responsa, 46*).

[135] When put together they read: "The exalted is [to be made] to sit down; he who humbles himself is [to be made] to be seen".

[136] cf. *Hilkhot Melakhim 11:3*. On the early diversity of Messianic expectations cf. Jacob Neuser, *"Judaisms and their Messiahs at the turn of the Christian era"*.

"HaShem will reign forever, your God, Zion, for all generations", and Rashi comments: "He will perpetuate his kingdom with the redemption of his children". Isaiah 35 (5-10) was interpreted in the same manner. Among the 1st century Qumran Scrolls there is an apocalypse that combines Psalm 146:6-7 with Isaiah 61:1 and attests, just like in the Gospels, that in the Messianic Redemption God "liberates the captives, restores the sight of the blind... heals the wounded, revives the dead and brings good news to the poor" (cf. 4Q521, F2). It seems Yeshua's number of miracles was so overwhelming that people began to believe because of them (Mt 11:23, 21:15; Jn 2:23, 3:2, 7:31) and this left the Sadducees perplexed (Jn 11:47).

We conclude, then, that while the official opinion is that Messiah does not need to perform miracles, it is sufficiently attested that the Gospels depict an authentic 1st century expectation concerning the signs of Redemption that existed in many Jewish circles of that time.

• The Nazarenes taught the theology of the **"resurrection of the dead"**. We take for granted that is something mentioned in the book of Daniel and therefore Scriptural, but most 'Sola-Scriptura' Jews in the first century did NOT believe in this doctrine. In their personal interpretation of the Bible, 'the resurrection of the dead at the end of times' is not mentioned anywhere. This shows how far a 'personal interpretation' can go when there is no Mesorah (i.e. Oral tradition). The resurrection of the dead stands as an 'Oral tradition' because it does not appear explicitly in the book of the Torah (cf. Matt 22:23-33; Sanh 90b; Antiquities 10:11.7).

• Paul (in 2Ti 3:8) mentions that **Yanes and Yamberes opposed Moses**. You will never learn who these two characters are from the Bible alone. Yanes and Yamberes is the name the oral tradition gives to the wizards who foretold the birth of Moses (Sotah 11a), emulated Moses' miracles during the plagues (Menakhot 85a), and became the leaders of the Erev Rav (ie. the mixed multitude) in the building of the golden calf (cf. Sefer haYashar; Onqelos; Zohar). Since Paul mentions their names from the oral tradition (names that do not appear in Scripture), it is obvious that the entire oral tradition goes with them, and not only their names.

• Shimon Keifa writes that: **"God did not spare the angels that sinned** [in Noah's time] but cast them down in chains of darkness" (2P 2:4). No need to say this does not appear anywhere in Scripture. Nevertheless, the source for this statement is a midrash in the Oral Torah, which states that in the time of the flood fallen angels (Uzza, Azael and their armies) came to the Earth and God bound them in chains of iron to a mountain of darkness.[137]

• Yeshua's disciple Yehuda (a.k.a Judas) says that **Enoch prophesied**, and he quotes the prophecy word by word (Jud 1:14-15). How can it be when the Torah does not record one single word from the mouth of Enoch? Can it be a quote from external literature? Yes, it is. Judas is directly quoting from Oral Tradition, and concretely from the 'Book of the Watchers' (cf. Hanokh 1:9); a mystical aggadah that tells the story of the fallen angels and Enoch's revelations in Heavenly realms. The tradition supports the idea that Enoch received hidden revelations while in the Upper Realms (cf. Shemot Rabbah 11:4, Bava Metzia 114b), and Kabbalistic literature also quotes Enoch (cf. Targum Pseudo Yonathan on Gn 5 & 6; Zohar I:37b; Sefer Heikhalot). It is appropiate to mention that the book of 'Enoc' has never been considered part of the Bible.

• In that same book Judas mentions a story in which **the archangel Michael contends with the devil** [ie. Samael] **for the body of Moses** (Jud 1:9). Once again, that is not written anywhere in the Bible. This is another oral tradition that has been mentioned in some ancient Jewish books (cf. Devarim Rabbah 11:6; Assumption of Moses 10).

---

[137] cf. Jubiless 5; Pirkei Eliezer 22; Zohar 3:208a.

• The Gospels talk about "**Hell**" and the "**Lake of fire**". The word "Hell" in the original is "**Gehenna**". Gehenna happens to be a Rabbinic word, from the Oral Torah. There is no mention of "Hell" (or Gehenna) in the plain text of Scripture. We could dig it out by some exegetical inferences such as the verse that speaks metaphorically of the Assyrian king's defeat: 'Since yesterday a bonfire has been prepared for the king' (Is 30:33), but as I said, in the literal level there is no mention of "Gehenna". The name is also absent in the Apocrypha.

As a matter of fact, the Sadducees - having the very same Bible – did not believe in Hell, so every mention of "Gehenna" in the New Testament is rooted in rabbinic oral tradition, and it would be ridiculous to assume that the Nazarenes spoke of the same place, with the exact same phraseology, but believed in a completely independent tradition.

• One of the greatest claims in the N"T is that **a righteous person** (in our case Yeshua) **can atone for the sins of the entire world with his suffering and death**.

Yes, the apostles deduced it from Isaiah 53, but the words of Isaiah had to be rooted in the Torah; otherwise he could be considered a false prophet. In fact, according to our most influential exegetes, Isaiah 53 - in its most literal meaning - talks about the suffering of Israel as a nation at the end of the exile, since the prophet continually calls them (Is 41:8; 44:1; 49:3): "Israel my Servant" and "Yaqov my Servant" (Rambam, Igeret Teiman; cf. Rashi & Ibn Ezra on Is 53; Targum Yonathan). The interpretation that identifies Isaiah 53's Servant with the Messiah or with a righteous person is essentially midrashic, and therefore, an element of oral tradition.

Yeshua said it is written in "the Torah, the Prophets and the Psalms" (Lk 24:44) but where is it written in the Torah? Nowhere! In the plain text there is nothing about it. On the contrary, quite often the counter-missionaries offer verses from the Torah that suggest that no vicarious atonement is possible.[138]

Yet, the sages of Israel consider it possible; but the whole concept is rabbinical in essence, and therefore, some clarifications are required:

(a) The word 'atonement' has more than one meaning in Judaism.
(b) They do not mean that if a righteous person dies, you have free access to the World-to-Come with no need to do your part. Quite the opposite: the death of the righteous opens for you the possibility to gain atonement by doing your part. This is the reason that the Gospel of Yeshua emphasizes the need to make penitence (Acts 3:19), because without repentance there is no atonement (Heb 10:26).

With this in mind, let us see what the Oral Torah says about it:

▫ "The death of the righteous atones [for the generation]" (Moed Katan 28a).

▫ "Rabbi Hiya Bar Abba said: The sons of Aaron died the first day of Nisan. Why then does the Torah mention their death in conjunction with the Day of Atonement? It is to teach that just as Yom Kippur atones, so also the death of the righteous atones" (Vayikra Rabbah 20:12).

▫ Following the previous statement: "Death and Yom Kippur atone when accompanied by penitence" (Yoma 85b [Mishna]).

"Why is the death of Miriam juxtaposed to the laws of the Red Heifer? This teaches that just as the Red Heifer brings atonement, so too, the death of the righteous brings atonement" (Moed Katan 28a).

▫ The Rabbis say: "[Messiah's] name is 'the leper', as it is written: Surely he has borne our grieves, and carried our sorrows: yet we did esteem him leper, smitten of God, and afflicted... Those of the house of the Rabbi say: 'the sickly', for it says: Surely he has borne our

---

[138] For example: Ex 32:33, Dt 24:16; Ez 18:20… etc.

sicknesses" (*Sanh 98b*). Also, the Midrash says: "I will take one of their righteous men and retain him as a pledge on their behalf, in order that I may pardon all their sins" (*Shemot Rabbah 35:4*).

▫ "True tzaddiqim atone for sins, as it is written (*Prov 16:14*): but the wise man will bring atonement" (*Likutei Moharan I, 7:4*).

The way the righteous one atones by his suffering and death is developed in different streams:
◊ He atones by the spiritual awakening that takes place after he passes away[139]
◊ He intercepts suffering that should fall on Israel[140]
◊ He makes corrections on higher and lower levels of the soul[141]
◊ He makes corrections on the world itself[142] (All ideas being present in the New Testament)

(7.4) Reminiscences of Mysticism

There are many more things in the Gospels as well as in the rest of the N"T[143] that are found in Jewish Oral Torah -- For instance, the expression (*Matt 7:3*): "Why do you look at the little twig in your brother's eye and pay no attention to the plank in your own eye?" [144] -- and others that belong to the Sitrei haTorah,[145] for example the trinitarian formula: Father, Son and Holy

---

[139] "The principal benefit that comes from the death of tzaddiqim is the spiritual and moral awakening that takes place after they pass away... In short, the death of tzaddiqim inspires us to imitate their personal conduct" (*Rav Kook, "Gold from the land of Israel", pp. 263-265*).

[140] "Know that while sometimes forgiveness of sins comes about through the collective merit of the community, there are times when the members of the community are not sufficiently worthy to have their sins forgiven in their own merit. The tzaddiq is then obliged to undertake to suffer for the sake of the Jewish people (*Is 53:4*): 'Surely he bore our diseases and carried our pains'. The community in general is saved from illness but not the tzaddiq, because he undertakes to suffer on behalf of the Jewish people" (*Likutei Moharan II, 8:6*).

[141] "One can receive [different soul levels] of a tzaddiq as an ibur (impregnation period that causes the soul's growth) and it will act as their [higher soul... to help them attain perfection] (*Shaar haGilgulim 2:4*).

[142] "Suffering and pain may be imposed on a tzaddiq as an atonement for his entire generation. This tzaddiq must then accept this suffering with love for the benefit of his generation, just as he accepts the suffering imposed upon him for his own sake. In doing so, he benefits his generation by atoning for it, and at the same time is himself elevated to a very great degree ... Such suffering also includes cases where a tzaddiq suffers because his entire generation deserves great punishments, bordering annihilation, but is spread via the tzaddiq's suffering. In atoning for his generation... he saves these people in this world and also greatly benefits them in the World-to-Come. In addition, there is a special, higher type of suffering that comes to a tzaddiq who is even greater and more highly perfected than the ones discussed above. This suffering comes to provide the help necessary to bring about the chain of events leading to the ultimate perfection of mankind as a whole" (*Ramhal, "Derekh HaShem" 2:3:8*).

[143] Like when Paul compares our perception of the World-to-Come with seeing from an opaque glass (*1Co 13:12*): "All the prophets gazed through an opaque glass, while Moshe Rabeinu gazed through a translucent glass" (*Yevamot 49b*); "the prophets could only grasp until the arrival of King Messiah; from here on they could neither grasp nor comprehend" (*Zohar 1:171a*).

[144] From the sages: "What is the import of the words (*Ruth 1:1*): And it came to pass in the days of the judging of the judges? It was a generation which judged its judges. If the judge said to a man: Take the little twig from between your eyes, he would retort: You take the beam from between your eyes" (*Bava Bathra 15b*).

[145] Sitrei haTorah (Secrets of the Torah) today called Kabbalah. In 1st century Maasei Merkavah uYetzirah were streams of mysticism based on the first chapters of Genesis and Ezekiel, passed down from the first Hassidim to the school of Hillel (cf. *Sukka 28a*).

Spirit (or Father Mother and Son),[146] the Ten Sefirot (which Paul names in order) (*Rom 11:33-36*),[147] ... etc. All of it exists in Judaism and is properly explained there.

Quite interesting is the fact that Yeshua was hanged on a tree, in a place named Golgoltha (the skull) (*Matt 27:33; Jn 29:17*). Many theories have been speculated, about the 5th century Golgoltha was even identified with a mount, but the truth is that in the first century there was no place called Golgoltha. More surprising is what some Fathers of the Church say about it: that it was called Golgoltha because according to Judaism the skull of Adam is buried there.[148] This idea is very peculiar because

(a) According to Judaism Adam's full body is buried in Hebron (*Sota 13a*).

(b) The only place where Golgoltha is mentioned in Judaism as the "skull of Adam" is in the mystical teachings of the sefirot, which are allegorically represented with human form (Adam Qadmon) and the skull of this anthropomorphic tree is the highest sefirah (called the skull of the Ancient One) from where the resurrection of the death will take place.[149]

Therefore, this Christian tradition is a reminiscence of an ancient Jewish mysticism which someone heard, misunderstood, and applied it literally to Adam, the first man.

---

[146] For the relationship of Father and Mother applied to God and the Community: *Berakhot 35b; Kidushin 30b; Bahir 104; Zohar II, 90a; Ramhal, "General Principles of the Kabbalah"*, p. 45. For the relationship between Mother and Son: *Sefer haPlia 4:2 (koretz 1784); Thomas 101, 105.* For the spirit of the community related to the Holy Spirit: *Shir haShirim Rabbah 1: 9 end; Vayikra Rabbah 35:7; Midrash Tanhuma, Naso 16 on Ex 25:8; sefer Yetzirah 1:9, Zohar Pequdei 221 [19], Mishpatim 2:97b [66].* For Holy Spirit being Mother: *Origen quoting 'the Gospel of the Hebrews' on Jn 2:12 and on Jer, "homily 15.4"; also Jerome on Micah 7:6.*

[147] cf. *1Chr 29:11.*

[148] *Origen on Matt n. 126, p. 13.*

[149] "From this Golgoltha trickles dew to the Exterior one [i.e. the Son], filling his head every day... from this dew the dead will rise as it is written: for your dew is dew of Lights" (*Zohar III:128b, Idra Rabba*).

CHAPTER 8: The debates about Shabbat

(8.1) So why attacking the Pharisees?

The logical question to ask is: If Yeshua is depicted as having the same theology, morals and teachings of the Pharisees, and lived among them, why his sharp criticism against them? Some have properly noticed that in the Gospel of John, Yeshua is a Pharisee:

(a) The Judeans in Jerusalem sent priests and Levites to inquire about John (*Jn 1:19*).
(b) Normally priests were Sadducees, but the text specifies here that these priests represented the Pharisees (*Jn 1:24*).
(c) The Baptist then says that Yeshua is one that stands among them – i.e. among the Pharisees (*Jn 1:26*).

Secondly, NOT all Pharisees had the same mindset (*Jn 9:16*). We have already seen that there were different schools of Pharisees and that there were sub-groups among them; even a group of them were believers (*Acts 15:5*). The reason this detail goes unnoticed is because – deprived of their historical and religious context – the Gospels seem to identify the Pharisees as Yeshua's natural enemy, to the point of being called 'sons of the devil' (*Jn 8:44*). But when we turn to historical and religious sources, it becomes clear that in general Pharisees were pious people, so this enters in conflict with the common Christian understanding.[150]

• The truth is that Pharisees were very critical with their own. For instance we read in their writings that the "Plague of the Pharisees brings destruction to the world" (*Sotah 20a [Mishna]*), that there are four classes that will not see the Shekhina (the Divine Presence after die): scoffers, liars, hypocrites and slanderers (*Sanh 103a*). Explaining the so called "Plague of Pharisees", they say that there are 7 kinds of Pharisees: Of these, five are considered hypocrites or fools, and the other two may be considered either good or selfish, depending on the point of view (*cf. Sotah 22a; Yerushalmi Berakhot 9:5*). The sages also said there were hypocrites who ape the Pharisees (*Sotah 22b*). Hypocrite Pharisees – they said – are "white pitchers full of ashes... whose inside is not like their outside" (*Berakhot 28a*). "They wrap their prayer shawls around them; they put tefillin on their heads, and they oppress the poor" (*Kohelet Rabbah 4:1*).

As you can see, the sages themselves attested that only one tiny portion of the Pharisees were perfectly good, so one must notice that when Yeshua harshly confronted the hypocrisy of the Pharisees, he was doing the same thing the "good Pharisees" did to their own.
The Gospels clearly reflect intra-Jewish disputes, between Jews with the same core beliefs, not between two different religions.
In addition, Pharisees loved "debating for the sake of Heaven". Quite often they would throw insults to each other, at times even hurting each other's feelings (*cf. Sanh 24a*), and at the end of the day they were best friends. The 1st century sages of Israel would insult their Babylonian neighbours with phrases such as: "foolish Babylonians who have dark opinions" (*Pesakhim 34b; Ketuvot 75a*). Despite the words, these were types of intellectual discussion, and their purpose was to increase the faith of the participants. As it is written: "Happy is the man who has his quiver full [of arrows]. For they will not be put to shame when they speak with their enemies at the gates" (*Psal 127:5*). Once Rabbi Tarfon harshly attacked Rabbi Aqiva, saying, "I can't take it any longer! Until when will Aqiva continue developing his worthless teachings?" A bit later he ends up agreeing with him and saying, "Rejoice, Abraham our father, that Aqiva came forth

---

[150] Nowadays the term Pharisee has become among Christians a synonym for 'hypocrite' and 'legalist'.

from your descendants. Whoever departs from the teachings of Rabbi Aqiva is as if he departs from his own life" (*Sifri Bamidbar*).

Now, I would like to rise a reasonable doubt. The Pharisees quite often invited Yeshua to have lunch at their home, and to learn from him. Why would they do this if they thought he was an heretic from another religious group? Pharisees did not waste their time inviting Samaritans or Sadducees to their homes because they already knew they were heretics. Would the Protestants waste their time testing the veracity of a… Mormon leader, for example? But about Yeshua one Pharisee says: "we [Pharisees] know that you are a teacher who has come from God" (*Jn 3:2*), and another one, Gamliel the elder, after naming other Pharisees with messianic expectations, says about the Nazarenes: "Leave them alone… lest you will be found fighting against God" (*Acts 5:39*). Do you think he would have said this if he thought that Yeshua and his group had an heretical theology, completely contrary to the principles of the Torah?

(8.2) the Holiness of the Torah

Here comes the problem: Unable to understand how Yeshua might very well be a Pharisee himself and at the same time attack them as he did, gentiles very early thought that Yeshua was·separating himself from Judaism and bringing forth a new religion. They see clear statements where Yeshua abolishes the dietary laws of the Torah, abolishes the observance of Shabbat, abolishes circumcision, and rejects the pharisaic traditions of ritual purification.

For centuries these Christians with such a distorted reality have tried to "convert" Jews. This caused the Jews to reject the Christian figure of Yeshua, and produced a need to defend themselves from 'replacement' doctrines and gentile assimilation. This defensive movement within Judaism is known as the anti-missionaries. There are serious quarrels between the two groups. Both interpret the New Testament with the very same lens, but the counter-missionaries turn the Christian teachings against them. They easily demonstrate that Yeshua, according to Christian theology, was an heretic unable to be the Jewish Messiah. And by Christian reasoning the counter-missionaries are totally correct, for the following reasons:

(a) **The Torah was given by God** – it is called the Torah of Moses because he was the mediator, but Moses did not write down his own ideas or philosophies; he just wrote what God told him to write – and this is stated in the whole Bible dozens of times. When people say that the Torah is not perfect, they are calling God imperfect.

King David said the Torah is perfect and has the power to convert the soul (*Psalm 19:7*) – which is contrary to Christian theology, as most Christians reject the idea that the Torah has the power to convert the soul.

(b) The Jew is permanently bound to the Torah in every generation: "And the statutes and ordinances, and the Torah and the commandment which he wrote for you, you shall observe all days" (*2K 17:37*). "Your Torah is truth" (*Psal 119:142*) and "His truth endures to all generations" (*Psal 100:5*).

(c) **"Sin"** is defined as **"Disobedience to God's Torah"** (*Lv 4:2; see Rom 4:15*). No one can come with their own definition of sin. Only the Torah defines Sin. Yeshua's disciples taught that 'Everyone who practices sin also practices lawlessness" (ie. lives without Torah) (*1Jn 3:4*).

(d) Yeshua said: Which one of you can convince me that I have sinned? (*Jn 8:46*) How could they know if he sinned or not? The only way is the Torah; Torah defines Sin. To claim that the Torah has been abolished is like claiming that we are now allowed to murder, which we are not.

(e) Therefore, Messiah must live according to the Torah and teach it (*Dt 17:18*). He who breaks or abolishes the Torah cannot be Messiah.

(f) Might one Jewish man appear out of nowhere making wonders, healing people, raising the dead, and saying he is the Messiah… but the Torah states that a true prophet is only the one who obeys and teaches Torah. If one prophet goes against Torah he is a false prophet (*Dt 13:1-4*). How can anyone say that Yeshua is the Messiah and at the same time try to justify their own theology, claiming that Yeshua broke or annulled the Torah? Only by ignorance.

(g) A very important rule of hermeneutics is that a verse cannot depart from its intended meaning. It can be interpreted with different lights, but not replaced with metaphors or spiritual fulfilments – which Judaism perceives as mere excuses. For example, if God tells you that you must dedicate the 7th day of the week to Him, he means it. You cannot say that the 1st day will do instead, because it does not do. Seventh is not first. This leads us to the topic of Shabbat.

Shabbat is part of the Decalogue (*Ex 20:8-11*), and one of the most repeated commands in the Bible. God even says that is a "perpetual covenant for the children of Israel for ALL their generations" (*Ex 31:16*). It is kind of grotesque when people say that the only thing they care of the 'Old Testament' is the Decalogue, but even then, they erase from the Decalogue the parts they do not like. If it is true that **Yeshua broke the Shabbat**, or taught others to put it aside, then he sinned. Period. So, is this true? Did Yeshua abolish all those things that Christians claim he abolished and/or replaced them with Spiritual fulfilments? I say no; rather, in all those accounts in which Yeshua seems to be contradicting Torah, actually what he is doing is debating his fellow Jews in internal disputes of Jewish law; *hallakha*.

(8:3) The Shabbat observance

Yeshua himself went to Synagogue every Shabbat (cf. *Mrk 1:21, 6:2*). When his students asked him about the destruction of Jerusalem, Yeshua told them to "pray that **your flight will not take place on Shabbat**" (*Matt 24:20*). This already testifies that Yeshua expects his disciples to keep Shabbat. Jews are forbidden to carry things outside of their area during Shabbat (cf. *Shabbat 73a*), so if they flee on Shabbat they would run away empty-handed – and that is the reason for Yeshua's warning.[151] Interestingly, many Christians interpret that this verse refers to a tribulation before the coming of Messiah; if that were the case, the verse alone is proof enough that the observance of Shabbat is still expected even today. When Yeshua died, the women who had come with him from Galilee rested on Shabbat "according to the commandment" (*Lk 23:56*).

"Therefore the people of Israel shall keep the Shabbat, observing the Shabbat throughout their generations, as a covenant forever. It is a sign between Me and the sons of Israel forever" (*Ex 31:16-17*).

• The book of Acts considers relevant to mention more than ten times that Yeshua's disciples gathered on Shabbat (cf. *Acts 13:14, 42-44, 16:13; 17:2; 18:4*). Nothing, absolutely NOTHING hints or implies that Yeshua abolished the Shabbat or replaced it with another day – which would be a violation of the Torah (cf. *Ex 20:10*).

---

[151] cf. *Rabbi Lichtenstein's commentary on Matthew.*

- As a matter of fact the scholarly evidence is that early Christians gathered on Shabbat as they had learnt from their original synagogue gatherings,[152] and independently also gathered on Sunday – which they called: "the 8th day" (which is a Jewish terminology for transcendence of this natural world. This natural world is based on patterns of sevens, and the 8th day is a shadow (reminiscence) of the World-to-Come).[153]

Some of the Fathers of the Church began to see Shabbat as unnecessary and spoke about it with rejection; some even came to speculate that "Sunday" had replaced it. Ignatius of Antioch (110 CE) for instance wrote:

> "If we live Judaism we confess not having received the grace... those who were brought up in the ancient order of things have come to the possession of a new hope, no longer observing the Sabbath, but living in the observance of the Lord's day"
> (*Letter to the Magnesians* 8).

Ignatius ignores that Paul did not impose the observance of Shabbat and circumcision on Greek believers, mainly because according to Jewish Law, gentiles are not obligated to observe these things;[154] it has nothing to do with abolishing the Torah.

One of the worst arguments for not observing Shabbat came from the putrid theology of **Justin Martyr** in his Dialogue with Trypho, who – for some reason that I cannot even begin to conceive – said that he does not observe Shabbat and the feasts because they were given to Israel "on account of your transgressions and hardness of heart... and unrighteousness" (*Dial. 18, 21*). Such was his biased perception of the Torah, without fundament, without understanding, contrary to the words of Isaiah (*58:13-14*). Sadly, many came to believe in a similar fashion.

Finally, in the Council of Laodicea (360 CE) Christians were directly forbidden to observe Shabbat, making it impossible for a Jew to become a Christian:

> "Christians should not Judaize and should not be idle on the Sabbath, but should work on that day; they should, however, particularly reverence the Lord's day and, if possible, not work on it, because they were Christians" (*Canon 29*).

Later Catholic doctrine makes it clear that Sunday became a replacement for Shabbat (a great violation of the Torah):

> "The Church of God has thought it well to transfer the celebration
> and observance of the Sabbath to Sunday"
> (*Cathechism of the council of trent; p 402, second revision*).

---

[152] "It is certain that the ancient Sabbath did remain and was observed – together with the celebration of the Lord's day – by the Christians of the East Church, above three hundred years after our Savior's death" (Edward Brerewood, "*A Learned Treatise of the Shabbath*" p. 77). "From the apostles' time until the council of Laodicea, which was about the year 364, the holy observance of the Jews' Sabbath continued, as may be proved out of many authors: yea, notwithstanding the decree of the council against it" (John Ley, "*Sunday a Sabbath*" p. 163).

[153] "We keep the eighth day [Sunday] with joyfulness; the day also on which Jesus rose again from the dead" (*Letter of Barnabas 15:6–8* [74 CE]).

[154] "Moses commanded us Torah; the inheritance of the congregation of Yaqov" (*Dt 33:4*) "It is our inheritance, not theirs" (*Sanh 59a*). A gentile must keep the Laws of Noah – and Shabbat is not part of them (*Sanh 56a-b, 59a*). He may take responsibility for additional commandments (becoming a Ger). A Ger who lives among Jews must commemorate Shabbat (cf. *Ex 20:10, Rashi, Kritot 9, Yevamot 40*).

The abolition of Shabbat is therefore a later Christian forgery, and not something that might have come from Yeshua, so let us see the disputed passages in the Gospels.

(8:4) Shabbat general arguments

Throughout the Gospels, certain Jews try to find fault in Yeshua and accuse him of breaking the Shabbat. Yeshua always defends himself with Hallakhic expositions. This modus-operandi is nothing rare among Pharisees:
In one occasion Rabbi Ullah visited the School of Pumbedita and saw the scholars shaking their garments [he thought, to remove the dust] and told them they were **desecrating the Shabbat**. Rabbi Judah replied that they were not stringent about it (*cf. Shabbat 147a; setama*). In other words, in the time when our Hallakha was being established (between 1st and 5th Century) it was common to find debates in which a Pharisee would accuse another in order to cause the other to expound Hallakha (the way to obey the commands). There was not a clear binding hallakha yet, hence there were many opinions.
That is exactly what the Gospels depict. The validity of the Torah is never in dispute; what is at issue is the proper way to obey the commands.

◊ It is written: "only, you must keep my Shabbat" (*Ex 31:13*). Our sages teach that the expression "only" (אך) in this verse is allowing for exceptions. Yonathan ben Yosef said, **Shabbat is committed to your hands, not you to its hand**[155] (*Yoma 85b*).
Yeshua uses a very similar expression: "Shabbat is made for man, not man for Shabbat, therefore the son of man rules even over Shabbat" (*Mrk 2:27-28; cf. Matt 12:8*). An almost identical statement is found in the words of our sages: "Shabbat was handed over to man, not man to the Shabbat" (cf. *Mekhilta Shabbeta I, on Ex 31:13*).
The above is precisely an important **Rabbinic principle** by which Shabbat can be relativized for the sake of people.

• One day he entered a synagogue and healed a woman, and the ruler of the synagogue accused him of working as a doctor on Shabbat (*Lk 13:10-14*); he called him hypocrite and demonstrated he was permitted to do so by a Rabbinic method of exegesis (*Kal vaKhomer*): if an ox can be untied on Shabbat to give it water, how much more a woman should be untied from what bound her! (*Lk 13:16*).

◦ Certain Pharisees accused him of breaking the Shabbat by healing a sick person. He replied to them, "Is it lawful... to save a life on Shabbat?" (*Lk 6:9*). The question is not rhetoric; his opponents knew that "Pikuakh Nefesh (ie. Saving a life) supersedes Shabbat" (*Yoma 85b*).

◦ In addition, our sages say (*Yoma 85b*): 'If **circumcision, which involves only one part of the body supersedes Shabbat, how much more the saving of the whole body**"! Interestingly, Yeshua used the exact same example: "If man receives circumcision on Shabbat... why are you angry at me for making a man['s body] whole on Shabbat?" (*Jn 7:23*).

• On another occasion, Yeshua's disciples were hungry and **picked some heads of grain**. They were accused of desecrating Shabbat (*Matt 12:1-2*). Yeshua then offered an example from Scripture in which a starving person -- namely, king David (*1S 21:6*) -- in order to save his life, violated a command and ate food that is only permitted to the priests (*Matt 12:5*). In few words, Yeshua was comparing both cases, admitting that his disciples violated Shabbat, but for a good reason; they were starving just like David. To eat raw grain indicates that they must

---

[155] It must be stressed that Rabbi Yonathan never meant to say that Shabbat is abolished, God forbid. He meant that there are exceptional situations where Shabbat can (and must) be neglected.

43

have been truly ravishingly hungry, as David was. In addition, they probably were fleeing from Herod, who sought to kill them.

◦ Now, interestingly, the example of David eating the showbread, is the VERY SAME example used by our sages when they decree that "every command of the Torah (except three) can be laid aside in times of danger"! (*Menakhot 96a*). The Mishna states: "Any matter of doubt as to danger to life overrides the Shabbat prohibitions" (*Yoma 8:6*). Coincidence?

◦ Later, Yeshua reinforces his argument with a teaching of the House of Hillel: "the sacrificial service [also] supersedes Shabbat" (*Shabbat 132b*). Immediately after this, Yeshua accuses his opponents of not having mercy (*Matt 12:7*). Why? Because knowing that his disciples were hungry, instead of providing food for them, they were there merely judging.

◦ Furthermore, in case someone wants to accuse them of stealing from the another person's land (which is not the reason the Pharisees discussed with them), the Torah allows the poor to take grain from the corners of the fields and leftovers of the reapings (*cf. Lv 19:10, 23:22; Mishna Peah*).

(8.5) the carrying on Shabbat argument

In the entire N"T, there is only one account where one might think that Yeshua actually broke Shabbat, and incidentally this account is in the Gospel of John. Since we have demonstrated that Yeshua and his disciples are positive about Shabbat observance, why would he actually break Shabbat in this case? Scholars who believe that the Gospels were composed in different theological stages[156] will easily dismiss John's account for betraying Mark's pro-Torah atmosphere and for gradually turning Yeshua into a non-observant Jew[157] (or directly a non-Jew). They would argue that this portion was a later thought interpolation, never written by any of Yeshua's disciples. This explanation is reinforced by the fact that the story itself contains verses that are undoubtedly interpolations, and because that would not be the only place in John where a later scribe incorporated an entire new chapter.

Still, given that the passage itself appears in every extant complete manuscript and is part of common Christian reading (and I believe Divine Providence is involved) I think there are different ways to deal with it, other than simply telling Christians to reject an entire chapter of John, which is a pill difficult to swallow.

• Yeshua went to Jerusalem to celebrate a Jewish festival, and somewhere not too far from the Temple there was a pool: Beit-Hasda (Bethesda), where lots of sick people gathered with the hope of being healed by the waters. [158] Yeshua went there on Shabbat and healed a man with the words: "rise, take up your mat and walk" (*Jn 5:8*).
Some Judeans then saw the man and told him that it is not permitted to carry things on Shabbat (*Jn 5:10*). From our hallakhic point of view they are right, since one of the few capital punishments of the Torah took place when a man carried sticks on Shabbat, after God had told them not to (*Nm 15:32; cf. Neh 13:19; Jer 17:21-22*). This leads us to believe that Yeshua commanded another person to desecrate Shabbat and therefore sinned.

---

[156] Such as Shmulei Boteach in "*Kosher Jesus*" or Hyam Maccoby in "*Jesus the Pharisee*".
[157] Hyam Maccoby argues that the account where Yeshua heals a leper and tells him to go to the priest at the Temple (*Mt 8:2-4, Mrk 1:40-44; Lk 5:12-14*) is suppressed in John precisely because it goes against John's depiction of a Yeshua owning no allegiance to Moses (cf. *Jesus the Pharisee ch 4, p. 43*).
[158] The interpolation says that an angel appeared, stirred up the water and healed the first one into the pool, but that was not part of the original text. It is more likely to be a pool dedicated to the Roman god Asclepius (the god of healing). The Mishna states that there were also pools dedicated to the goddess Fortuna (*Zavim 1:5*).

However, this is not the whole picture and there are many contextual factors that must be addressed before making such an accusation. After all, our sages taught that we must judge every person favourably (*Avot 1:6b*).

◦ Firstly, we cannot stress enough that a 1st century Jew should not be judged according to our modern standards. In the 1st century our Hallakha was still being debated and the Pharisees argued with each other even about Shabbat details.[159] The Gospels insinuate differences between the Galilean and the Judean observances.

◦ Even though carrying objects out of your place is a Shabbat transgression, Pharisees are known for finding ways to circumvent the issue without altering the Torah, similar to how politicians make new laws without altering the constitution.

The Jewish Law says that one cannot carry or transfer things into a public domain on Shabbat,[160] but it also describes what constitutes a public domain and what is considered a private or unitarian domain (**Reshut haYakhid**). According to the description, the pool was surrounded by 5 covered colonnades (*Jn 5:2*), thus implying that the place was surrounded by **Tzurat haPetakhim** (doorframes) and therefore was considered a communal area in which people could carry things on Shabbat, although maybe in that time some people disagreed.

◦ The way to by-pass the Shabbat prohibition is by raising an **Eiruv**[161] around the area. The Gemara tells us that "Jerusalem would have been considered a **Reshut haRabim** (a public domain) if its city-gates were not closed at night" (*Eiruvin 6b*), and then Rashi[162] explains that the custom was to surround the city with an Eiruv – hence everyone in Jerusalem could freely carry objects on Shabbat.

◦ Rashi might be right and the entire Jerusalem was surrounded by an Eiruv, or maybe that specific place was surrounded by the Eiruv of the Temple area, or by the symbolic Eiruv created by the five covered colonnades, this being the reason why John bothers to describe in detail the area in which this incident took place (*Jn 5:2*). In this case, Judeans would have noticed he was about to leave the boundaries of the Eiruv and were warning him not to do so while carrying his mat. If that were the case, Yeshua did not violate Shabbat, because he simply told him: "Carry your mat and walk", but walking beyond the Eiruv with the mat was the man's doing. Another alternative is that these Judeans were perhaps Sadducees who did not believe in the validity of the Eiruv.

◦ Notice from the context how those Judeans did not care for one second about the miraculous healing, but were only troubled with technicalities, condemning the healer and the healed (they were what we call: radical legalists). Yeshua might have set aside all the technicalities of their Judean neighbours purposedly, and out of mercy told the sick man to "pick up his mat", because he was an indigent who needed it to sleep at night, thus being part of Yeshua's wider understanding of **Pikuakh Nefesh** (saving a life); after all, the Judeans opinion was not hallakhically binding.

◦ Verse 18 says: "Therefore the Judeans sought the more to kill him, because not only profaned Shabbat but also said that God was his father, making himself equal to God." This verse reflects the point of view of those Judeans, and not necessarily Yeshua's real behavior. They wanted to kill him because they "thought" he broke the Shabbat. It would be wrong to side

---

[159] "The laws of the Shabbat limits are only Rabbinical" (*Eiruvin 59a*).

[160] cf. *Jer 17:21; Lv 34:21; Nm 15:32; Nehemiah 13:15-18, 10:31. cf. Shabbat 6a, 14b, 96b; Eiruvin 21b, 22b; Arukh Hayim 363:1.*

[161] A Jew cannot walk more than 4 cubits out of his area on Shabbat and cannot carry things in a public domain (*cf. Eiruvin 41b [Mishna ch 4]*). An Eiruv is a rabbinic enclosure of the neighbourhood – whether literal or symbolic – that transforms a public domain into private, thus allowing freely walking and carrying things (nowadays the whole city of Jerusalem is enclosed with an Eiruv).

[162] *Rashi on Eiruvin 6b*; cf. *Tosefta Pesakhim 66a*. The tradition of the Eiruv is so ancient that the sages attribute it to Solomon (cf. *Shabbat 14b*).

with them; Yeshua didn't break Shabbat, it's a false accusation, and should it be true, then he sinned.

(8.6) The Ones behind the plot

The last thing that must be noticed is how the Gospels depict Pharisees desiring to kill Yeshua for his Shabbat healings. As some scholars[163] argue "Pharisees wishing to kill Yeshua for preaching a Pharisaic doctrine make no sense". So they speculate that probably in the re-edition of the Gospels the name 'Pharisees' was substituted for the original 'Sadducees', because it was the Sadducees who in general were more legalists and literalists on Torah observance and, after all, the ones who sentenced Yeshua to death were the Sadducees. From the mouth of the Pharisees, 'a tribunal that executes even one person in 70 years is a murderous court' (*Mishna Makkot 1:10*). This does not fit the Christian preconceived ideas.

However, given that there were so many different types of Pharisees, one must conclude that when the Gospels refer to "The Pharisees" cannot – and do not – mean "ALL the Pharisees"; even in context the logic is absurd. Rather, there was a group of Pharisees who had corrupted themselves, and in their desire to have a first-class position, associated themselves with the Herodians (Hellenistic Jews who also worked with Sadducees),[164] as it is inferred from the following verses: "And the Pharisees… took counsel with the Herodians against him, how they might destroy him" (*Mark 3:6*), "beware of the leaven of the Pharisees and of Herod" (*Mark 8:15*), "And they sent to him certain Pharisees and Herodians to catch him in his word" (*Mark 12:13*), but other Pharisees were not the same, as it is written: "that day some Pharisees came and told him: Go and flee from here because Herod wants to kill you" (*Lk 13:31*).

How could we ignore the fact that in the false trial many false accusations were brought against Yeshua (*Mrk 14:56*), but desecrating Shabbat – which would have been a good excuse for his execution – was not even mentioned? In fact, in the same manner that John the Baptist was executed for giving the nation Messianic hopes (*Antiq. 18:5.2*), the sole reason Yeshua was sentenced to death was because he threatened the Pax Romana[165] (the Roman peace cf. *Jn 11:50*) by proclaiming himself 'King of the Jews' which for the Sadducees threatened the peaceful authority they enjoyed under Roman rulership, and for the Romans was an attempt of sedition,[166] a crime punished with crucifixion.[167] The high priest had already determined that in order to save the entire nation (from the harsh Roman reprisals) Yeshua had to die (*Jn 11:50*). The trial was only the excuse for the execution and had nothing to do with the Torah. I think the use of *"Sunhedrion"* (*Matt 26:59; Mr 14:55*) in this context can be misleading.[168] Sunhedrion means a 'joint session' or tribunal (cf. *Matt 5:22*); not necessarily the main court of justice; i.e. the Great Sanhedrin of 70 sages. The Gospels say that the Romans were involved in the arrest (*Jn 18:12*), that the trial took place in Qayapha's house, not in a court of justice, and that he was not judged according to Jewish Law. For example, it is forbidden to judge someone at night or at

---

[163] Hyam Maccoby *"Jesus the Pharisee"* ch 10, p. 125.

[164] A similar scenery is depicted with Paul, who being a Pharisee, joined the Zealots and worked for Sadducees.

[165] One might argue that his crime was that of blasphemy, but then he should have been lapidated under Jewish law, but instead he was hanged on a tree, under Roman law (cf. *Mishna Sanhedrin 3:4*). The farce began by accusing Yeshua of instigation against the Temple, and it ended with a proclamation of blasphemy that is not so. The charge of blasphemy yelled by the Sadducee high priest was a blasphemy against Rome not against God, as they later proclaim: "we have no other king but Caesar" (*Jn 19:15*). Proclaiming oneself Messiah (or any synonymous title, such as son of God) is not any crime under Jewish Law. In fact, there is a Talmudic account where each school considers their Rabbi to be Messiah.

[166] "Any challenge to Roman authority, any challenge to the peace of Rome, would have been met with a swift and violent response" (Michael White *"From Jesus to Christ"* part I).

[167] *Josephus, "Antiq." 20:6.2, "Wars" 2:12.6.*

[168] Peshitta uses '*Kanusta*' כנושתא which means 'synagogue' and/or 'assembly'.

Passover's eve. Giving a fellow Jew away to the gentiles is a sin known as "the selling of Yosef", which not even the school of Shammai would have done. Obviously, if Yeshua was in fact a blasphemous, and the accusation had been justified, the Sanhedrin would had decreed or asked for his lapidation (something that rarely happened, since the sages always looked for legal loopholes and reasonable doubts before sentencing someone to death). Therefore, accusing the sages of killing Yeshua is a big mistake. Gentile powers infiltrated in a corrupt group of Jews (which is called "Erev Rav" – the mixed multitude) were responsible for the killing of the Nazarene (Lk 18:51), and the process was led by the Judean Sadducees (Mr 15:3, 10).

My final observation: Our sages said that the book of Esther was written with careful words and without an explicit mention of God for fear of their oppressive government. The choice of harsh words in the Gospels against Pharisees and the sweetened silence about Roman cruelty may have been the result of a similar scenery.[169]

---

[169] A silence that is not absolute, as Luke dares to reveal that Pilate had mingled the blood of some Galileans with the blood of their sacrifices (Lk 13:1). All the historical sources attest to the fact that Pilate was in Judea with the sole purpose of keeping order at all costs, and any threat against his authority was quickly eradicated. His hand was especially severe with Jews and Samaritans (cf. Josephus, Antiquities 18:4:1-2, 18:3:2). It is therefore surprising from a historical point of view that in the Gospels Pilate refused to execute Yeshua (Matt 27:18; Lk 23:14; Jn 19:12), although it is still possible that this was the case. After all, Pilate was a real person and just like every real person, he could have had his good moments as well.

CHAPTER 9: Hand-washing and Dietary Law

(9.1) different approaches for the same story

Some Pharisees came from Jerusalem questioning Yeshua about his disciples, wondering why they break the rules of the elders by eating food **without washing their hands** (*Matt 15:2*). There are three major points of view for this text, I call them: "the Christian", "the Karaite" and the "Orthodox" approach. In my opinion, none of them is completely 100% satisfactory, as there is still "something" missing in the wholeness of the hermeneutic reading of the text.

The question: "why your disciples break **the tradition of the elders**" seems to imply that they are in fact referring to a Pharisaic tradition known as "**Netilat-Yadaim**" (the ritual washing of hands before meals). In fact, Mark's version explains with a very neophyte language the Judean tradition of washing themselves many times before eating (*Mrk 7:3*).

(a) In "**the Christian**" interpretation Yeshua opposes the Pharisees for substituting the word of God with their man-made traditions; they are only preoccupied with legalistic rules, while Yeshua only cares about the inside. Yeshua says that nothing that enters from outside can contaminate the body, and therefore from that moment on, all foods became clean; i.e., the need to observe the dietary laws of the Torah ceased. So this Christian approach ends up with the surprising conclusion that Yeshua is giving us green light to eat any kind of food (even pork or seafood); since "what goes into the mouth does not defile the man" (*Matt 15:11*). In other words, Yeshua is depicted as rejecting the traditions because they go against the Law, and then he rejects the Law itself and replaces it with his own personal point of view.

(b) "**The Karaite**" approach, similarly states that Yeshua was rejecting the man-made traditions as a whole, because they always invalidate the written text of the Torah. Thus Yeshua quotes: "they worship me in vain, for their teachings are but rules taught by men". In short, the Karaite approach advocates for Sola-Scriptura – but we have already seen in the previous parts of this essay that he was anything but Karaite.

(c) "**The Orthodox**" approach is contextually more plausible, makes more sense and it is the necessary bridge into a correct interpretation. 'The Orthodox approach' simply questions the other two points of view and ends up with the conclusion that Yeshua was teaching a moral lesson, not necessarily going against the tradition. Let us see their 7 arguments:

- **(1)** First of all, how can a debate whose main subject is the 'purity and defilement' by washing the hands end up condemning kashrut (ie. the laws of permitted foods)? It does not make any rational sense and does not follow the logical flow of the narrative. The permission to eat forbidden foods is not even considered here – the rules of hermeneutic do not allow for such a deviation from the context in such a manner.
- **(2)** Why would Yeshua contradict himself, first saying that everyone who teaches against the Torah will be called the least in the Kingdom of Heaven (*Matt 5:19*), or accusing those Pharisees of violating the Torah with their man-made traditions, and then a few verses later he allows his Jewish disciples to eat what the Torah forbids? It does not make any sense.
- **(3)** How can Yeshua contradict God and teach his disciples to sin? [since the Torah defines Sin]. Messiah is supposed to come to do the will of He who sent him (*Jn 6:38*). A

Messiah that contradicts God is NOT a Messiah, but a false prophet (*Dt 17:1-5*). Those who pick and choose which command to obey and which command to ignore, of them it is written: "they have cast away the Torah... and despised the word of the Holy One" (*Is 5:24*). Therefore, did he really, with one single phrase, get rid in one stroke of all the Laws of kashrut? Very unlikely.

- **(4)** How can Yeshua contradict himself, rejecting the Netilat-Yadaim and then telling his disciples to "do and observe everything the scribes and Pharisees tell you to do"? Isn't it inconsistent?

- **(5)** About the phrase: "**what goes into the mouth does not profane a man**", could it mean that foods forbidden by the Law are now permitted? Certainly not, since we can prove that Yeshua's own disciples refrained from eating such food – for example, when **Shimon Keifa** received the vision of the great sheet in which there were all kinds of beasts, reptiles and birds (*cf. Acts 10:11*) and a voice told him: "kill and eat", Shimon answered and said: "NO WAY, Master, I have never eaten anything that is common or unclean" (*Acts 10:14*). This he said having been with the Master for three years and after the Master rose up from the grave. If Yeshua really taught that we can eat forbidden animals – why was Peter unaware of it? Peter (who in that moment had just finished his daily prayer and was very hungry *cf. Acts 10:10*) did not hasten to eat the first thing he found; on the contrary, he meditated on the meaning of the vision – he was convinced it WAS NOT LITERAL (*Acts 10:17*) – and finally, he found out that the vision did not have to do with food at all, but it was a metaphor for the acceptance of gentiles into the community of Israel (*Acts 10:28*).

- **(6)** Is not the text clear enough when at the end we read (*Mark 7:19*): "**This [he said] making all foods clean**"? Not at all. On the contrary, that is a mistranslation and sadly in some Bibles [such as the NIV] the phrase is completely changed, modified and falsified as to say that 'by saying these things Yeshua declared all foods clean – even those foods that the Law forbids'. But that is not a logical conclusion for the discussion at hand. Now, the idea that something is called 'food' implies it is edible. Many of you would not eat rat, or human meat or a car's wheel – you will say that is not edible. In our context, all the audience is Jewish and the food that is being discussed is bread. For these Jews a dog, for example, is not edible; nor a pig, nor shrimps – and they are, therefore, excluded from the context as they are not considered food.

- **(7)** The moral of the story[170] is in Yeshua's words: "**eating with unwashed hands does not profane the man**" (*Matt 15:20*). This means that the food is unclean only because God render it to be unclean but it is not intrinsically unclean. There is a similar phrase from our sages: "The dead does not make you unclean, nor the water makes you clean [just because is water]; but rather it is a decree that the Holy One has decreed [and thus, it is God's law what makes these things defile or purify you]" (*Bamidbar Rabbah 19:8*).

I would say the "Orthodox approach" solves most contextual and hermeneutic problems, but in its last clause it puts aside the still problematic fact that the main reason for the debate is that, indeed, some of Yeshua's disciples "did not wash their hands". Yeshua's final point of view is that there is nothing wrong with eating without performing the hand-washing, something that the Orthodox approach evades. Now let us bring the story back to its historical and religious context.

---

[170] *cf. Profiat Duran, Kelimat haGoyim 24-25; cf. Rashbatz, Kesher uMagen.*

(9.2) two things to notice

In the 1st century the Hallakha was not monolithic.[171] Pharisees had their differences concerning purity regulations. There was a fellowship known as the Khaverim: they adhered to the purity laws in ways that go beyond what the Jewish Law establishes, almost as meticulously as the High Priest (cf. *Mishna Hagiga 2:7*). There was the opposite side as well: a great majority of Jews who did not observe the purity laws more than what the Torah requires. The Khaverim called them: Am-haAretz (people of the land) and in their opinion they were ignorant.[172] Another example: most Pharisees ruled that liquids that had been left in the open should be thrown away as they might be contaminated by snake poison – something common in that time (*Mishna Teruma 8:4*), while the Charismatic Pharisees (also called Hassidim) opposed to this view because they thought it shows a lack of faith in God (*Yerushalmi Taanit 23a*); the others replied that one should not rely on miracles for the things that are for us to do[173] (*Qiddushin 39b*).

Second consideration: being 'ritually unclean' does not equal sin. Uncleanness only becomes sin when a person brings this uncleanness into the realm of what is forbidden. For instance, one becomes unclean by burying a corpse which is not a sin; it is actually required in order to bury it. A woman becomes unclean by having Niddah (menstruation), and that is not a sin. One can become unclean by touching a leper, and it is not sin. But if they are in a status of uncleanness and enter in the Temple contaminating the priests' consecrated food with their hands, then they sin. You can have an unclean animal as a pet (such as a dog) and it is not sin, but if you eat it, then you sin. Therefore, something unclean is something that cannot have a status of holiness (i.e., cannot be set apart) for the Divine Service.

(9.3) explaining the Netilat-yadaim

Originally the '**ritual washing of hands**' together with the washing of feet was something commanded to the priests before starting their service (cf. *Ex 30:18-21*) and before they touched the terumah (the donations and tithes that Israel submits to the priests *cf. Lv 22:7*). Terumah belonged to the Temple – i.e., to God (*Lv 22:15*) – so it could not be profaned. An ancient tradition states that in the first Temple Solomon decreed that the priests must perform Netilat-Yadaim before touching sacrifices (Qorbanot) as well, as to remind them the holiness of the place (*cf. Shabbat 14b-15a; Maharsha*). **This Netilat-Yadaim was an act of holiness**, not of hygiene (*Lv 22:2-3*). Even if the priest was already clean, he had to ritually wash his hands before doing anything. It was a ritual ablution, not sanitary: just like the baptism (tevilah) for repentance or for woman's purification after menstruation.

Shammai and Hillel required every one of us, priests and Israelites, to wash hands before eating bread, in order to familiarize the priests (*cf. Hullin 106a*). According to Rashi, the only reason Jews perform the netilat-Yadaim is to ensure that the priests will wash for the terumah

---

[171] In fact, even today (when Hallakha has been codified and standardized) it is not yet as clear as some people hoped it would be. After the era of the sages, Rambam, in an attempt to preserve homogeneity during the Diaspora, tried to codify the Hallakha in the 'Mishne Torah' and Raavad spoke harshly against him, saying that codifying it is destroying its spirit. Later, Yosef Karo tried to do the same in the Sulkhan Arukh, and even today there is a tiny debate between those who follow Rambam and those who follow Yosef Karo. Also, there are those who follow the Tosafot (addendums), and those who do not. If this is true in modern times, then can you imagine the 1st century atmosphere of debates?

[172] cf. *Mishna Demai 2:3; Gittin 5:9; Pirkei Avot 2:6, 5:10*.

[173] There are similar ideas in the N"T: Yeshua says not to worry for the tomorrow; occupy yourselves with the Kingdom of God and his righteousness and the rest will be added to you. And Paul says: He who does not work, does not eat.

[something that will be important when the Temple be rebuilt][174] and Smag says in addition that the sages pretended to encourage cleanliness and holiness.

> "Why was the defilement (*tumah*) imposed on un-rinsed hands? It is because a person's hands are active (and apt to touch parts of the body and many dirty things) and then when he touches the terumah (i.e., consecrated food), it will be rendered inedible"(*Shabbat 14a*).

How did it become part of Jewish Law? The **Netilat-Yadaim** was one of the 18 ordinances adopted in accordance with the School of Shammai the day of the zealots' seizure, when they killed students of Hillel in order to outnumber him and impose Shammai ordinances.[175] "But it was not accepted from them" – the sentence: "it was not accepted from them" means that since the citizens were not observing this practice, it was annulled – because a decree that the nation does not accept upon themselves does not stand.[176] A generation later "their students re-established it and it became accepted" (*Shabbat 14b*). Not too much after that time, Rabbi Aqiva performed Netilat-Yadaim in prison, with the little water he had, in order not to contradict the decree of the majority [even though he was not necessarily in agreement to it] (cf. *Eiruvin 21b*).

Yeshua's years of ministry are in between the two periods. This means that **there was no Netilat-Yadaim established by Hallakha during Yeshua's ministry** – at least not in the way we think about it today, and in case there was, it was being imposed by the Shammai students; not by Hallakha. The 'Washing of Hands' debated in the Gospels is a more 'religious-sanitary' and less 'religious-ritualistic' version (which developed later), as the context confirms [and it is Rashi's point of view as well]. Yes, in addition to ritual traditions the sages established sanitary traditions, like the one we have mentioned above: the prohibition to drink from certain liquids if they remain uncovered for the fear that a snake may have left some venom in it (*cf. Terumot 8:4*).

(9.4) exploring the text

It is notorious that the Pharisees in our story **came from Jerusalem** (*Matt 15:1*), so they were Judeans, which implies a difference of customs between the two communities, because let us remember that Yeshua was a Galilean. Our sages recorded difference of opinions of this kind; e.g. Isaac ben Ashian was of the opinion that washing hands before meals was a meritorious act but not an obligation, and actually, the halakha in the Tosafot goes according to this opinion (cf. *Hullin 105a; Tosefta Berakhot 5:14*). What if Yeshua and his community did not see it binding either? They are still representing one important sector of the Pharisees!

• The second thing to notice from the story is that **only "some of his disciples"** and not ALL of them ate without washing hands (*Mark 7:1-2*). This means that the rest did, in fact, wash their hands, and it is also worth noting that **Yeshua was not accused here**, which implies that he did wash his hands. One might say there is a similar story in the book of Luke in which Yeshua is questioned for "not washing himself before eating" (*Lk 11:38*), but in this case the "hands" are not mentioned, and the verb used in the manuscripts implies that the Pharisee was expecting Yeshua to bathe himself before eating – something that is too exaggerated even for Pharisees.

---

[174] cf. *Magen Avraham O.C. 158; Rashba*.
[175] cf. *Shabbat 13b, 17a; Yerusalmi Shabbat 1:4*.
[176] cf. *Yerusalmi Shabbat 1:4; Rashi on Avoda Zara 36b*.

- Opening the debate, Yeshua does something very common in Rabbinic expositions: he answers their question with another question, and then offers his point of view.
    - (a) **The question he raises** (*let me paraphrase*): how you dare to accuse my disciples of breaking a tradition when you guys are doing far worse, breaking commands of the Torah through your traditions? (*Matt 15:3*).
    - (b) **The point of view he offers**: the food enters and goes out… it does not defile the man if you eat it with unwashed hands[177] because all food passes through the stomach and is purged… but the things that come out of the mouth come from the heart (that is, the evil thoughts), and these defile a man" (*Matt 15:17-20 / Mrk 7:19*).

Since the text implies that Yeshua did wash his hands (as also did some of his disciples), to say that he was totally contrary to washing his hands (as the Karaites stress) does not satisfy the context. The "Orthodox approach" makes more sense here as it deduces that Yeshua is opposing hypocrisy – namely, the hypocrisy of those who are so pedant that dare to judge others while at the same time they do worse things, having forgotten to fear their God.

Carefully observe that Yeshua brings to their attention one specific tradition: the one in which a Pharisee denied his possessions to his parents through a vow, with the excuse that **his goods are a Qorban (offering) to God**. Yeshua said this goes against 'honor your father and your mother' (*Matt 15: 4-6*). It is only after this example that Yeshua accuses them to follow man-made rules learned by rote (*Matt 15:9; cf. Is 29:13*). This tradition of transforming a vow into a Qorban is discussed in the Mishna, in tractate Nedarim:

There is the case of a son who wanted his father to participate in his wedding, but his father was forbidden to benefit from his son because of a vow. The son then gave all the possessions of the ceremony to a third party [thus making him the owner of everything] with the intention that his father could participate, but the third party consecrated it all to Heaven and the son lost it all (cf. *Nedarim 5:6*).

For the Jews vows are serious business. To the sages these kind of vows are technically permitted under the command of the Torah: "he must do everything that came out of his mouth" (*Nm 30:3*), however, such a person would be embarrassed and considered wicked – since only a wicked person would make such a vow in which he does not need to honor his parents (cf. *Nedarim 1:1, 9:1; 64b*). The sages thus taught: "Do not swear at all… [Unless he wants to be nazarite or the like] the righteous does not make vows".
This is relevant with what Yeshua says after this, that the "evil speeches" come from within, and defile the man. In other words: the son who denied his possessions to his father in order to make them a Qorban to God is considered a wicked son, because he did not think of honoring his parents; he should not have made such a vow in the first place, for it defiled him.

◦ Yeshua refutes their position of "external" defilement by accusing them of "spiritual" defilement. Those Pharisees were saying that if you eat without washing your hands, dirtiness will enter your body and it will defile you. He says that cannot be the case, because what you eat (as long as it is not poisonous or sinful) is purged by the body through excretion (that is how God arranged the body). Thus the original text reads this way:

---

[177] This applies to the School of Shammai, and it might apply to all the Khaverim, who didn't eat with Am-haAretz (common people or sinners) because they didn't want to get ritually unclean. Even in the N"T Shimon Keifa refrains from eating with gentiles in Antioch after Jewish men sent by Yaqov the Just came to make him a visit (*Gal 2:12*).

> "Don't you see that nothing that enters a man from the outside can
> defile him? Because it doesn't go to his heart but into his stomach, and
> then out of his body **thus purging all foods**" (*Mark 7:18*).

This is confirmed by the parallel passage in Matthew 15:17, "Do you not understand that everything that goes into the mouth passes into the stomach and is eliminated?" then he adds: "what defiles a man are [his sinful thoughts and lusts], but eating with unwashed hands does not defile a man" (cf. *Matthew 15:19-20*).

∘ Oftentimes you will find the house of Shammai debating over external matters, such as: 'we have to pray the shema reclined' while Hillel would say: it does not matter, as long as you direct your prayer toward God (cf. *Mishna Berakhot 1:3*). From all of the above we can deduce with no shade of doubt that Yeshua's words are participating in a bigger debate that took place in the 1st century, dealing with different points of view about the "washing of hands" and in his approach and exposition he reflects the kind of points of view you would expect from the house of Hillel.

CHAPTER 10: The heirs of Yeshua's theology

(10.1) the ancestors

According to Judaism the ones who are authorized to interpret Torah in a practical level - the arbiters of God's word - are the Jewish sages of Israel. The Torah must be interpreted according to their methods of interpretation and the Jewish Law must go in each generation according to their decree. "To them belong the oracles of God". The beginning of tractate Pirkei Avot lists a chain of reception for the Torah, which also serves as the chain of authority; starting with Moses himself up until the sages of Israel (i.e. the scribes and Pharisees):

> "Moshe received the Torah from Sinai and transmitted it to Joshua [i.e. Yehoshua]; Joshua to the elders; the elders to the prophets, and the prophets transmitted it to the men of the Great Assembly [which had been instituted by Ezra]... Shimon the Righteous was among the survivors of the Great Assembly... Antigonus of Sokho received from Shimon the Righteous... Yose ben Yoezer and Yose ben Yohanan [the first Zugot] received the tradition from them... Yehoshua ben Perakhia and Nittai of Arbel received from them... Yehuda ben Tabbai and Shimon ben Shatakh received from them... Shemaya and Avtalion received from them... Hillel and Shammai received from them" (*Pirkei Avot 1:1-12*).

The Samaritans had their own line of reception, and the Sadducees (*Tzeduqim*) traced their line of authority back to Tzadoq; the first high priest in Solomon's Temple, descendant of Eleazar, son of Aaron[178] (*1K 2:35*). Did Yeshua confirm any of these lines of reception? Or did he reject them all and imposed a new line of tradition? In other words: which community represents him and his theology best?

Yeshua rejects the Samaritan tradition when he says: "salvation is of the Jews". In his conversation with the Samaritan woman one can notice that he thinks of the Samaritan faith as a corruption of the Torah, and as a matter of fact, his love for the Temple goes against the Samaritan faith.
Yeshua rejects the Sadducees, calling them ignorant of the Scriptures (*Matt 22:29*); he believes in the resurrection of the death as one of the basic principles of the Torah, while mainstream Sadducees do not. Again, a wrong theology.
How about the Pharisees? It is true that Yeshua told his disciples to beware of the "leaven" of the Pharisees and Sadducees (*Matt 16:6*). In the Matthew account Yeshua does not explain the parable to the disciples, and they "understand" that the leaven is the doctrine (*Matt 16:12*). The key word here is "understand", because (a) Pharisees and Sadducees have not the same doctrine, and (b) in Luke's account Yeshua DOES explain the parable, and what he means is their hypocrisy; not their theology (*Lk 12:1*). In fact, Yeshua vouches for the Pharisees' authority to teach and interpret Torah (notice how he does not include the Sadducees in this verse):

> "The scribes and the Pharisees sit in Moses' seat,
> so you must do and observe everything they tell you to do" (*Matt 23:2*)

The straightforwardness and clarity in this verse is such that non-Jewish scholars find it troublesome for their theology and many times have attempted to distort its plain meaning. For instance, most of the Christian commentators and apologists focus on the next verse,

---

[178] cf. *Abraham Geiger, "Urschrift" p. 20.*

which says: "But do not do according to their works, for they say but do not do" (23:3). They simply evade the previous verse, acting as if it does not exist. I have debated with Messianics and Karaites who think that the 'Matthew Shem Tov' – which they claim to be the original Hebrew of Matthew – does not say: "they [the Pharisees] tell you" but rather "he [Moses] tells you", but such a claim in unauthentic and absurd. Firstly, because the claim that they sit in Moses' seat implies by necessity that they represent Moses. Obedience to Moses goes hand in hand with obedience to those who sit in his seat. Secondly, because their 'Matthew Shem Tov' is not the Hebrew original; it is not even ancient: it is a medieval reinterpretation included in a larger book (Even Bohan) written by a Jew named Shem Tov Ibn Shaprut. Thirdly, because all the thousands of manuscripts of Matthew, whether in Greek, Latin, Hebrew or Aramaic… ALL of them say the very same thing in this verse, INCLUDING six of the nine manuscripts of 'Shem Tov's Matthew'.

• **"They sit in Moses' seat"** – It is written that "Moses sat to judge the people" to "teach the statutes of God and his Torahs [*torotaiv*]" (*Ex 18:13, 16*). Yitro told him it is not good to "sit" alone to judge (*Ex 18:14, 17*), so he suggests organizing a group of sages who would rule the nation in the name of Moses (*Ex 18:21-22*). Interestingly, it is customary even today to stand up when reading from the Torah, and to sit down to interpret it or to make judgment. The fact that it says "they sit" already implies oral interpretation.

• **"You must do and observe everything they tell you to do"**. The source for this is the verse: "*Al pi haTorah asher yorukha*" – "on the Oral [explained, spoken part] of the Torah which they will direct you… you must do, and do not decline neither to the right nor to the left" (*Dt 17:11*). Yeshua is unmistakably referring to Deuteronomy, and his mention of scribes and Pharisees substantiate the fact that he accepted the legitimacy of the Pharisees' authority to interpret Torah as seen in the Pirkei Avot lineage. As a matter of fact, the very same teaching is found in the Oral Torah:

> "Do not say: I won't obey the words of the sages because they are not
> in the Torah. The Blessed Holy One says: No, my son, but everything
> they tell you to do, do it, because it's written: On the Oral Torah
> which they will direct you" (*Pesikta Rabbati 3*).

Putting things in perspective, even if most of them are a bunch of hypocrites, the Torah gives them the authority to interpret the Bible and to establish the laws of the Jewish nation. It is no a mere coincidence that after the destruction of Jerusalem the Sadducees and the Essenes faded away, but the Pharisees remained. It is as if Yeshua knew it would happen.

"If your righteousness does not exceed that of the scribes and Pharisees in no way you will enter into the Kingdom of Heaven" (*Matt 5:20*). This verse can be explained in at least two positive ways: First, notice that "Kingdom of Heaven" does not mean "going to Heaven after death" (that is a Christian theology that was developed later). The Kingdom of Heaven refers to the sovereignty of God on Earth; therefore, like the Hassidim, a Jew is expected to go beyond the letter of the Torah (to be more righteous than the Pharisees) in order to bring the Messianic era (i.e the Kingdom of Heaven). Another explanation is that, since he was talking to common people, many of them sinners, he was expecting them to return to God and become pious people (cf. *Lk 15:10-32*). About this our sages teach that the righteousness of a repentant sinner (a Baal Tshuva) is way bigger than the one of a man who in general has never sinned.[179] This is also stated by Yeshua, when the Pharisees ask him why does he eat with sinners, and Yeshua replies that those who are Ok do not need a physician, but the sick ones do (*Matt 9:10-13*). With these words he was suggesting that those Pharisees were Ok. Yeshua

---

[179] cf. *Hilkhot Tshuva 7:4*.

reproaching the Pharisees and raising a bigger standard of holiness is also in line with the Jewish tradition that when Messiah comes, he will cause even the righteous ones to repent (*Zohar III:153b*).

(10.2) on this Rock I will build my church

We have seen that Yeshua vouches for the authority of the sages in matters of Torah interpretation and Jewish Law, based on the Torah itself. We have seen in the first chapters of this essay that Yeshua's theology is imbedded in the Judaism of his time and therefore the later Christian theology does not represent him. Yet, Catholics claim their Papacy are the heirs of Yeshua's authority on earth, and they prove it with an unbroken line of succession that goes directly to Keifa (whom they call Saint Peter). After Shimon bar Yonah declared that Yeshua is the Messiah, he said *(Mt 16)*: "**You are Keifa**[180] **and upon this rock I will build my community**".

Most Protestants understand that the Rock Yeshua is referring to is Keifa's statement that 'Yeshua is the Messiah' and that Christianity as a whole has the keys of heaven to bind and to loose, thus replacing the previous authority that Judaism held.

The Latin Church understands here that Yeshua is naming Keifa 'head and major authority of a new Church'. Keifa is the one who has the keys of the kingdom to bind and to loose, and this is supported by a second verse: "feed my sheep" *(Jn 21:26)*.

By tradition Peter is believed to have died in Rome, so they claim that he is the first Roman Pope and, therefore, founder of the Papal lineage by Yeshua's command.[181]
Basically, we could sum up their belief in their own Papal lineage on three foundations:

1. Peter is the chief Apostle, the first Pope according to Yeshua.
2. Bishops are the successors of Peter.
3. Since Peter died in Rome, Roman Bishops are the maximum representatives of Yeshua on Earth.[182]

Bishop means overseer; what we call in Hebrew Paqid or Mashgiakh.[183] During and after the apostles' ministry on earth there were bishops (i.e. overseers) taking care of each community and each city. For instance, Paul wrote two letters to Timotheus, who was the overseer (bishop) in Ephesus *(1Ti 1:3)*. A bishop in Rome was not bigger or smaller than a bishop in Edessa. In fact, the headquarters of the believers was in Jerusalem. There we read in the book of Acts and in Paul's letters (Gal 2:9) that the heads of the Community were three:

-   **Yaqov** haTzaddiq (Yeshua's brother, a.k.a James).
-   **Keifa** (a.k.a Peter).
-   **Yohanan** (a.k.a John).

◊ The first thing we notice is that the New Testament says nothing of Keifa becoming a maximum authority in Rome; on the contrary, the few biblical references point us to the fact

---

[180] Keifa means rock in Aramaic.

[181] "The holy Roman church has been placed at the forefront not by conciliar decisions of the churches, but has received the primacy by [the verse]… "You are Peter"… In addition to this… the most blessed apostle Paul… by their own presence and by their venerable triumph they set it at the forefront over the others of all the cities of the world." *(Decree of Damasus I, part 3 (382 C.E).*

[182] cf. *Canon 3 of Sardica.*

[183] Mashgiakh Rukhani; Spiritual overseer; also called Menahel or Mashpia – or in Aramaic Sa'or – refers to a Jewish overseer; the ancient title was Paqid (overseer) [*Neh 11:9*] which can be a Jewish authority or the responsible for a Noahide community as well (cf. *Acts 20:28*).

that his activity was focused on Jerusalem, Babel and Asia Minor. Besides, Paul – who spoke of the overseers in Rome – never mentions Peter among them (*cf. Rom 16*).

◊ The second issue is that even if Keifa stayed and died in Rome, that does not make Rome any better than Jerusalem or any other city where the disciples also stayed and died;[184] that is the Roman Church making enormous assumptions out of thin air.

◊ The third matter to consider is that according to Acts, the voice of the community was Yaqov and not Keifa (*Acts 12:17, 15:13*).

The Gospel of Thomas – which shows in many ways a pre-Gospel tradition – supports the Acts and Galatians account by saying:

> "The disciples said to Yeshua: We know that you will depart from us. Who is to be our head? Yeshua said to them, wherever you are, you are to go to Yaqov the righteous, for whose sake heaven and earth came into being" (*Thomas #12*).

(10.3) the Christian papal lineage

Although we are looking for the heirs of Yeshua's theology, I do not see the necessity to explore or to test the traced-back-to-Moses Rabbinic lineage any further, because **(a)** there are no alternative lists in Jewish literature and **(b)** Yeshua himself testified of its validity, as seen above. As per the Papal lineage, given all the above: its innovation, its replacement of Jewish and even of Torah authority, its non-Jewish theology… etc, we must scrutinize it carefully. Nowadays, the chronological order of the Popes has been canonized by the Church and is not questioned; everyone learns the same list of Popes in the Pontifical Yearbook, but this is far from being historical information, since this catalogue is based on the Liber Pontificalis (6th century onwards) and the Catalogus Liberianus (4th century), whose information about the first 18 Popes is gathered from Christian traditions and legends, and not from history books. Anyway, the beginning of the Papal lineage is as follows:[185]

1 – Peter (Shimon)
2 – Linus
3 – Anacletus (Cletus)
4 – Clement
5 – Evaristus (Aristus)

It all supposedly began with Keifa, who transmitted his authority to Linus.
Apparently Linus was succeeded by Anacletus of Rome (also called Cletus), who transmitted his authority to Clement of Rome. Now let us explore some interesting facts:

---

[184] "How Peter died is not told in the New Testament. Later legend would fill out the details of Peter's life and death in Rome… [including] his crucifixion upside down in the Vatican Circus in the time of the Emperor Nero. These stories were to be accepted as sober history by some of the greatest minds of the early Church: Origen, Ambrose, Augustine. But they are pious romance, not history, and the fact is that we have no reliable accounts either of Peter's later life or of the manner or place of his death. Neither Peter nor Paul founded the Church at Rome, for there were Christians in the city before either of the Apostles set foot there. Nor can we assume, as Irenaeus did, that the Apostles established there a succession of bishops to carry on their work in the city, for all the indications are that there was no single bishop at Rome for almost a century after the deaths of the Apostles. In fact, where ever we turn, the solid outlines of the petrine succession at Rome seem to blur and dissolve" (*Catholic historian Eamon Duffy, "Saints and Sinners: A history of the popes" 4th edition, chapter I, pp 2-6*).

[185] cf. *Annuario Pontificio (i.e. Pontifical Yearbook)*.

(a) While most accounts claim it all began with Peter alone, Irenaeus claims that the foundation of Rome's authority comes from two apostles: Peter and Paul, who founded the most ancient Roman church and passed the leadership to Linus.[186] But that is not true. The church of Rome was obviously not so ancient as those of Jerusalem or Antioch, nor was it actually founded by Peter or Paul (cf. Rom 15:22).[187]

(b) Irenaeus claims[188] that Linus is the same one mentioned in the New Testament, but the fact is that the name Linus appears only once in the New Testament and has no connection with Peter whatsoever (2Ti 4:21), making Irenaeus a good storyteller, but nothing else.

(c) Not even one of the details given about Linus' life can be historically confirmed.[189]

(d) In Clement's letter there is a brief mention of Peter, Apolos and Paul, but no mention whatsoever of Linus or Anacletus, or any other Bishop prior to him.

(e) Neither Ignatius mentions any Bishop called Linus or Anacletus.

(f) Tertulian does not mention Anacletus and in his list, Clement goes after Peter.[190] Jerome does basically the same thing.[191]

(g) Hippolytus mentions Clement first, then a certain Cletus and then Anacletus (which it was supposed to be the same as Cletus, but in this case it is not).

(h) The Liber Pontificalis says that Cletus was a Roman, a Bishop in the days of Vespasian, and Anacletus was a Greek, in the days of Domitian (but other sources say they are one and the same).

(i) As a matter of fact, T.J. Campbell, in the Catholic Encyclopedia says that the only thing we know of Anacletus is that he ordered a great number of clerics. That is to say that anything else has probably been invented, and hence the so many different versions of the Papal lineage. The Papal lineage has been fabricated.

(j) Linus, the so claimed successor of Peter, was not named 'Bishop of Rome' until one century after his death and was not considered a 'Pope' until late 4th century.

The first mention of the title "Pope" dates back to Egypt and was applied to the Bishop Heracles of Alexandria (232 C.E). From the early 3rd century the title "Pope" was a common designation for any bishop in the West. The title Pope was not reserved exclusively for the leader of Rome until late 11th century.[192] Historians guarantee that there has not been Popes in Rome prior to Siricius of Rome[193] (c. 384), at least not as a Supreme Pontiff.[194] In other words: Neither Anacletus, Linus, or Keifa were Popes (not as Supreme Pontiff anyways).[195]

Even the Catholic scholar John O'Malley wrote:

> "The Christian community at Rome well into the second century operated as a collection of separate communities without any central structure... Rome was a constellation of house churches, independent of one another, each of which was loosely governed by an elder. The communities thus basically followed the pattern of the Jewish synagogues out of which they developed"
>
> (O'Malley JW. "A History of the Popes" p. 11).

---

[186] cf. Adversus Haereses, III:3.2,3.

[187] Sullivan F.A. "From Apostles to Bishops: the development of the episcopacy in the early church", p. 147.

[188] Adversus Haereses III:3.3.

[189] Scholar J.P. Kirsch admits this in the Catholic Encyclopedia about Linus.

[190] Clement, "De praescriptione, xxii".

[191] Jerome, "Illustrious men 15".

[192] Jonh O'Malley, "A history of the Popes" p. xv. Cf. Thomas H Greer "A brief history of the western world" p. 172.

[193] Bettenson & Maunder, "Documents of the Christian Church" p. 88. cf. Lopes A. "The Popes: The lives of the pontiffs through 2000 years of history", p. 13.

[194] Lat. 'Pontifex Maximus'; a title that designated the maximum authorities in the pagan cults of Mithraism, later adopted by the Latin Church for the Roman Pope.

[195] cf. Lopes p. 13.

In other words, Roman Bishops evolved with the time into Popes. "Probably there was no single 'monarchical' bishop in Rome before the middle of the 2nd century... and likely later".[196] For the 5th century onward, the Pope in Rome was completely considered the 'heir of Peter' and representative of Yeshua by the Catholic Church. The Pope was not only heir of Peter, and not only representative of Yeshua... but in the 7th century the Pope became the 'Vicar of God'! He became some kind of religious emperor whose decisions could not be questioned. Interestingly, this Pope was invested with far more authority than Peter himself had in the New Testament.

(10.4) the truth of 'binding and loosing'

These were the facts so far. "Passing of the keys of the kingdom" to Keifa was never a monarchical imposing measure of authority. Peter was a community member who consulted with other apostles and even was sent by them (cf. *Acts 8:14*). Keifa always worked in team with Yohanan (*Acts 3:1-11; 4:1-22; 8:14*). And Paul even dared to confront him when he was wrong (*Gal 2:11*); from which account we learn that Yaqov was in a higher position than Keifa (*Gal 2:12*).

The truth is that the famous Rock in Matthew 16 is not Peter, but the proclamation that 'Yeshua is the Messiah', as even the early fathers of the church testify,[197] and the entire community – not Peter alone – has the power to bind and loose. Now this expression must be understood in its proper Jewish context:

'**Binding and loosing**' - i.e. allowing and forbidding (*Matt 16:19*) – is a rabbinical legal term that refers to posqim (deciders of the law), who have the duty to decide the legal process for a situation where the Hallakha has not been established yet, and for what to do with the sinners and heretics of the community they rule (cf. *Hagiga 3b*).[198] Just as each community had their posqim, Yeshua's community must have their posqim. It is clear that Yeshua did not mean Keifa alone when he gave permission to bind and loose, for this appears in other parts of the Gospels where Yeshua speaks to the entire community and not to Keifa alone (cf. *Matt 18:18; Jn 20:23*). The common evangelical interpretation in this rule is off-track, for they think that "binding and loosing" refers to demons. The Catholic interpretation is closer to Jewish interpretation in the sense that the posqim could, indeed, excommunicate people, proclaim a fasting day, or decide what to do with the gentile believers that come to them (*Acts 15:3, 28*) – in other words, they can decree the rules of their community (which they call "church")[199] – but

---

[196] *Cambridge History of Christianity, volume 1, p. 418.*

[197] "Of all the fathers who interpreted these passages in the Gospels (*Matt 16:18; Jn 21:17*)... not one of them whose commentaries we possess – Origen, Chrysostom, Hilary, Augustine, Cyril, Theodoret, and those whose interpretations are collected in catenas – has dropped the faintest hint that the primacy of Rome is the consequence of the commission and promise to Peter!... they understood by it either Christ himself, or Peter's confession of faith in Christ; often both together. Or else they thought Peter was the foundation equally with all the other Apostles (cf. *Rev 21:14*)" (*Catholic historian von Dollinger, "The Pope and the council" 74*).

[198] "Under Queen Alexandra... the Pharisees... became the administrators of all public affairs so as to be empowered to banish and readmit whom they pleased, as well as to loose and to bind" (Josephus, *"Jewish wars" 1:5.2*). They could for instance 'bind' a day by declaring it a fast day (*Taanit 12a*). When the opinions of different schools differed (especially – but not only – the schools of Shammai and Hillel) it was common to hear the words: "One binds (i.e. forbids) and the other looses (i.e. allows)" (cf. *Megillah 26b, Pesakhim 3a, 36b-37a; 55a [Mishna]*); and Yeshua himself may refer to the School of Shammai when he says "they 'bind' heavy burdens but won't move them with one finger" (*Matt 23:2-4*).

[199] The term "Church" does not appear in the New Testament; the word Ekklesia simply means community or assembly, and although it might refer to different groups within Judaism, or even synagogues, it does not refer to something separated from Judaism, as later Christians interpreted.

the Catholics are mistaken in one of the most important principles: The posqim cannot override the rules of the Great Sanhedrin; that is, in matters that have become obligatory (i.e. have been bound on earth, and therefore have been also bound in Heaven).[200] Neither can the posqim invent a new religion; and most importantly, they cannot, just as the Great Sanhedrin itself cannot, override or contradict the Torah of God.[201]

As for the idea that the Jerusalem community abolished circumcision, that is just a mere misinterpretation of what the book of Acts states. The Jerusalem Council did not decide anything on the validity of Moses' Law; what they decided was the way to deal with this new phenomenon: A wave of gentiles who came to shelter under the wings of the Shekhina. Acts states that there were a group of believers among the Pharisees who thought that the new members could only be "SAVED" (i.e. make it to the world-to-Come) if they were circumcised and completely submitted to the 613 commands of the Torah (*Acts 15:1, 5; Gal 6:12-13*). They wanted all believers in Yeshua to be Jews. The Jerusalem council said that such a command did not come from them (*Acts 15:24*) and decreed that circumcision will not be imposed on former heathens, i.e. believing gentiles. They do not need to become Jews and obey the 613 commands of the Torah. Later Paul would develop that salvation does not come by having a Jewish identity (i.e. by circumcising). In the whole story, the community is dealing with gentile new members, not with Jews. It does not say anywhere that a Jew must not circumcise his son anymore. In fact, Paul is accused of abandoning the Torah and vouching for paganism (*Acts 18:13; 21:28*), and he defends himself against this accusation. Keifa himself says that many twist the words of Paul because he speaks things difficult to understand (*2P 3:15*). And finally, let's not forget that the Nazarene community was divided into "those sent to circumcision (i.e. Jews) and those sent to un-circumcision (i.e. gentiles)" (*Gal 2:7-9; Acts 10:45*).

The Jerusalem community therefore binds on the new gentile-believers only four requirements: to abstain from **(1)** idol contamination **(2)** fornication **(3)** strangled and **(4)** blood. These four are not the whole law that a gentile must observe, but as they say: "It is my judgment that we should not make it difficult for the gentiles that are turning to God" (*Acts 15:19*). The four categories are things that could scandalize their fellow Jews at the synagogue, and that can be found in Leviticus 17:12 – 18:21.

(1) Idol contamination: "Do not give any of your seed to set them apart to Molekh, do not profane the name of your God" (*Lv 18:21*).
(2) Fornication: "Do not uncover the nakedness of…" (*Lv 18:6-20*) "You shall not lie with…" (*Lv 18:22-23*).
(3) Strangled: "in hunting any beast…" (*Lv 17:13-15*). "Any tool that strangles the animal by not allowing its blood to be spilled is not valid for slaughter" (*Hullin 1:2*).
(4) Blood: "No soul of you shall eat blood" (*Lv 17:12*).

There are those who say that abstaining from blood refers to murder. This is not so, because gentiles already had laws that prohibited murder, and the community had no need to regulate that. Obviously, if they regulated murder, they should have included many other things in the list, such as robbery. The "blood" reference is plainly and clearly a prohibition of eating blood (a common practice among the gentiles which is forbidden by the Torah).

---

[200] There were sanhedrins for each tribe and each town, and even a specific Sanhedrin of priests, and certainly each community had their own courts of Justice (being the minimum established a set of three judges per community), but they were all submitted under the Great Sanhedrin of 71 members (*Sanhedrin 16b; Mishna Sanhedrin 1:6; cf. Ex 18:21, 24:9; Dt 16:18; cf. Mishna Ketuvot 1:5*).
[201] *Dt 4:2*. For instance, the sages take for granted that Hillel could not change the law of the Sabbatical year (*Gittin 36a*). Ramban (*on Dt 4:2*) explains that a Rabbinic prohibition will sometimes be set aside in the face of conflict with a Torah one.

And how do we know these laws apply also to gentiles? Because in the same portion is written:

> "Because with all of these the nations that I cast out before you have contaminated themselves" (Lv 18:24).

Since these things corrupt even the gentiles, the disciples considered that these four laws were a good place to start dealing with them, in what back then was a 100% Jewish community. Those new believers would learn more Torah at their local synagogue, as the verse says: "For Moses has been preached in every city… and is being read in the synagogues on every Shabbat" (Acts 15:21).

The procedure taken by the Jerusalem community of not imposing conversion to Judaism is in harmony with what our sages call the "Seven Laws of Noah".[202] As they taught: "a Gentile who pursues the study of Torah is like a high priest – that refers to their own 7 commandments" (Sanhedrin 59a), meaning that gentiles do not need to observe the Laws of Jewish identity such as circumcision. He who gets baptized and circumcised for the sake of Torah becomes a Jew, and is obligated by Law to observe all the commands of the Torah (cf. Gal 5:3). But as long as he remains a gentile, he has (so to say) certain privileges that are not permitted to the Jew.

(10.5) Paul of Tarsus

I conclude recalling that if the Jerusalem community did, in fact, abolish circumcision for the Jews, then they sinned and are nothing but heretics.[203] Many would want to refute my claim through the letters of Paul. What Paul said or did not say in his letters is another topic, I firmly believe that his letters have been largely misinterpreted by the masses and taken out of their historical context, in addition to having been highly edited by pagan scribes.
His letters were never intended to be the Biblical Canon of a new religion.
Paul makes it clear that he speaks according to his knowledge, sometimes emphasizing that he is offering his own personal opinion. "I don't speak by command… I offer you my opinion on this matter" (2Co 8:8-10). Paul himself makes the difference between the commands of the Torah and his own commands, attesting that the words of the Torah are more important. "To the rest, I say, not the Lord… " (1Co 7:10-12). And on another occasion: "Concerning the virgins I have no commandment of the Lord, but I give my own opinion" (1Co 7:25).

Paul dares to say something even more radical: "Let me talk, not from the Lord, but as a foolish, in the certainty that I have something to boast about" (2Co 11:17).

Furthermore, Paul's preachings are not infallible. Occasionally he makes mistakes, like when he mentions those who died in the plague of Midian and says there were 23,000 dead people (1Co 10:8), but the Torah says there were 24,000 (Nm 25:9), which is attested even in the LXX.
Besides, did the different communities really receive Paul's letters as coming from God's mouth? (1Ts 2:13) Not all of them. Paul himself rebukes a community because there were among them those who preferred to listen to Paul, others preferred Apollos, others Keifa, and others preferred none of them (1Co 1:11-13). These preachers were far from being perceived as Biblical prophets. Many of Paul's letters were lost because people did not take care to protect them. How could all of this be compared to the Holy Writings of our Biblical Prophets? At best, the letters of Paul have the value of theological correspondence between a teacher and his

---

[202] "In the 28 jubilee Noah began to enjoin upon the sons of his sons the ordinances and commandments, and all the judgments that he knew" (Yovel 7:20).
[203] Not to mention that Paul would be seen as an hypocrite for circumcising Timothy (who was son of a Jewish woman) (Acts 16:1-3).

different students, (as it has been the case of many Rabbis who left us entire epistles, which were written exclusively for members of their community or for specific disciples). Paul's literature has been canonized and explained without taking into account that each individual letter had a different context and dealt with specific issues for specific people.

I have not even begun to touch the subject of Paul; this is much more extensive and it requires an essay on its own. In order to avoid making this essay any longer, let us simply remember that anyone who calls himself a "Follower of Yeshua" should live according to "Yeshua". If Paul, for whatever reason, contradicts or appears to contradict Yeshua, then you should follow Yeshua and not Paul.

Blessings

-Xus Casal

APPENDIX to Chapter 7.4: Paul's enumeration of the sefirot

Romans 11:33-36

KETER	Oh, the depth of the riches	
KHOKHMA	of the wisdom	
BINA	and knowledge of God!	
GEVURA	How unsearchable his judgments,	*(judgments are attributes of gevura)*
HESED	and his paths beyond tracing out!	*(God's paths are Hesed – Psalm 25:10)*
TIFERET	Who has known the mind of the Lord? Or who has been His counselor?"	*(Tiferet is related to the other emotive sefirot. Following the previous Psalm, God's paths are Hesed and "Truth", emet = Tiferet)*
NETZAKH	"Who has ever given to Him,	
HOD	that He should repay them?"	*(Netzakh and Hod function as conductors; they are called the tactical sefirot: giving in order to receive. Hod represents retribution)*
YESOD	For from him and by him and in him are all [kol] things.	*(Another name for Yesod is "kol", all)*
MALKHUT	To him be the glory for ever.	*(The glory in reference to the shekhina and the congregation responding "Amen" are both Malkhut characteristics)*

שַׁעַר י"ב

פרק ראשון

אלה תולדות יש"ו בן
דוד בן אברהם

אברהם הוליד את יצחק ויצחק הוליד את יעקב
יעקב הוליד את יהודה ואחיו

הוליד את פרץ ואת זרח מתמר פרץ הוליד את חצרון
חצרון הוליד את רם ורם הוליד את עמינדב
את נחשון ונחשון הוליד את שלמון שלמון הוליד את
בעז בעז הוליד את עובד מרות עובד הוליד את
ונובד הוליד את ישי ישי הוליד את דוד עוד הוליד
את נתן שלמה המשך אגדה שלמה הוליד את
רחבעם רחבעם הוליד את אביה אביה הוליד את
אסא אסא הוליד את יהושפט יהושפט הוליד את
יורם יורם הוליד את עוזיה עוזיה הוליד את יותם יותם
הוליד את אחז אחז הוליד את חזקיה חזקיה הוליד את מנשה
מנשה הוליד את אמון אמון הוליד את יאשיהו